To my mother:

You've always wanted me to be an author, and had you not encouraged a love of books onto me, I would not have been who and where I am today.
I love you.

TABLE OF CONTENTS

Publish a Book Like a Boss

The Fast Guide to Selling on Amazon

Written, designed and created by Sherry

DISCLAIMER

Although the author and publisher have made every effort to ensure that the information in this book was correct at press time, the author and publisher do not assume and hereby disclaim any liability to any party for any loss, damage, or disruption caused by errors or omissions, whether such errors or omissions result from negligence, accident, or any other cause.

COPYRIGHT © 2020 Sherry of *Save. Spend. Splurge.*

In accordance with the *Canadian Copyright Act*, the scanning, uploading, and electronic sharing of any part of this book without permission of the publisher constitutes unlawful piracy and theft of the author's intellectual property. If you'd like to use the material from this book (for purposes other than for reviewing), prior written permission must be obtained by contacting **Sherry** (*www.likeabossbooks.com/contact*).

Thank you for your support of the author's rights.

Sherry@LikeABossBooks.com

@saverspender

INTRODUCTION

Me? An author? If you had told me I'd be writing books and enjoying it years ago, I would have laughed in disbelief. I honestly thought publishing a book would be the hardest thing in the world. How would I get an editor? A publisher? I didn't know the first thing about it.

Then, when I ventured out with my first book, I made a lot of mistakes along the way. Then I wrote a second book and realized I could have saved myself a lot of of trouble, money and heartache of if I had a read a book like this one beforehand. So here it is. Don't make the same mistakes I did.

P.S. — Drop me a line any time, I'd love to hear from you!

Sherry@SaveSpendSplurge.com

Edit

Shape

Publish

1

2

3 4

5

Tools

Other

EDIT

Breathe

It helps. It doesn't matter where your book is at right now - completely done with chapters, or just in a first draft, but take a break and breathe. When you're not so caught up in it (give it 24 hours), and then revisit it.

Ask yourself a few questions:

- What is my core message?
- Did this core message resonate throughout the book?
- Does it make sense when I read through the book and it flows?
- If it is an educational book - Can I group this into teachable sections?
- Is there anything in there that doesn't need to be?
- Are there parts good as a follow-up or supplemental book?
- Is it too long and unwieldy to read? Will people lose interest?

Consider

Other things you might want to consider using to break up the book or to tell the story better if it is educational/informative is graphs, images or anything visual.

I myself an am visual learner, so if you're teaching me something, I would like an image for my brain to rest on or to pick apart in lieu of words.

Check

Have someone else proofread it, or else you need to be extremely sure that your spelling, grammar, punctuation and facts which is why taking a break is key because when you're too into the book, your eyes can miss things.

Keep it neat

Try and keep the paragraphs and text as neat as possible, meaning in shortish paragraphs for easy reading, but also without a lot of spaces in between.

This is obviously an author-style thing as well, maybe your writing is just like this, but keep in mind that things that are too long and too short, can be difficult to read when it becomes a sea of words or disjointed thoughts:

Example of a too-long paragraph:

> *Lorem ipsum dolor sit amet, consectetur adipiscing elit. Pellentesque id dictum neque. Aliquam in ex nisl. Pellentesque habitant morbi tristique senectus et netus et malesuada fames ac turpis egestas. In pulvinar condimentum aliquam. Praesent ut nunc in sapien tempus cursus ut at magna. Maecenas felis eros, lobortis cursus rhoncus id, pharetra vitae sapien. Etiam pulvinar elementum erat, vitae consectetur sapien posuere sed. Vestibulum dignissim, nisi vitae fringilla auctor, erat risus laoreet magna, non volutpat purus ipsum eu lacus. Morbi at ultricies lectus. Phasellus quis convallis velit. Phasellus mollis turpis ac mauris egestas, in viverra magna ultrices. Vestibulum vitae fermentum odio, vitae dapibus lectus. Nulla ut metus lacinia, elementum dui sed, fringilla ante. Integer quis dignissim risus. Ut lorem lacus, egestas nec arcu vitae, aliquet semper mi. Curabitur eu suscipit nunc, sed aliquam eros. Aliquam porttitor tortor eget nunc bibendum ornare. Nam efficitur urna interdum neque aliquam, sit amet euismod nisi vehicula. Pellentesque condimentum sollicitudin dapibus.*

Too long. It needs at least 3 paragraph breaks to give the thoughts a break, and time to breathe in the reader's mind.

Example of a single sentence with too much spacing:

Lorem ipsum dolor sit amet, consectetur adipiscing elit.

Pellentesque id dictum neque. Aliquam in ex nisl.

Pellentesque habitant morbi tristique senectus et netus et malesuada fames ac turpis egestas.

In pulvinar condimentum aliquam.

Praesent ut nunc in sapien tempus cursus ut at magna.

Maecenas felis eros, lobortis cursus rhoncus id, pharetra vitae sapien.

Etiam pulvinar elementum erat, vitae consectetur sapien posuere sed.

Vestibulum dignissim, nisi vitae fringilla auctor, erat risus laoreet magna, non volutpat purus ipsum eu lacus.

Morbi at ultricies lectus.

This could be an instance of too much spacing and unless it is to emphasize some bullet points of some sort, or a list, it can be difficult to read.

Example of a good paragraph with enough spacing:

Lorem ipsum dolor sit amet, consectetur adipiscing elit. Pellentesque id dictum neque. Aliquam in ex nisl. Pellentesque habitant morbi tristique senectus et netus et malesuada fames ac turpis egestas. In pulvinar condimentum aliquam. Praesent ut nunc in sapien tempus cursus ut at magna.

Maecenas felis eros, lobortis cursus rhoncus id, pharetra vitae sapien. Etiam pulvinar elementum erat, vitae consectetur sapien posuere sed. Vestibulum dignissim, nisi vitae fringilla auctor, erat risus laoreet magna, non volutpat purus ipsum eu lacus. Morbi at ultricies lectus. Phasellus quis convallis velit. Phasellus mollis turpis ac mauris egestas, in viverra magna ultrices.

Vestibulum vitae fermentum odio, vitae dapibus lectus. Nulla ut metus lacinia, elementum dui sed, fringilla ante. Integer quis dignissim risus. Ut lorem lacus, egestas nec arcu vitae, aliquet semper mi. Curabitur eu suscipit nunc, sed aliquam eros. Aliquam porttitor tortor eget nunc bibendum ornare. Nam efficitur urna interdum neque aliquam, sit amet euismod nisi vehicula. Pellentesque condimentum sollicitudin dapibus.

Easy to read, simple to follow and clear. Even these paragraphs halved, would look better and be easy to read.

SHAPE

Table of Contents (TOC)

Keep it simple and easy.

You don't want your TOC to be messy, full of detail and information. I'd suggest the 3-Level Rule, as in no more than 3 sets of headers. I personally only use two because a lot of information in the TOC can either be useful or overwhelming - you make the decision.

There are ways to make text as highlighted headers or titles without having to make them formatted as Headers for your TOC (as in, to not have them show up) as well.

Alternatively, you can always do this manually by typing out each title, then tab-spacing the subtitles but that's a lot of work for nothing when you have tools as your disposal.

Copy and paste your entire book into one of the 6x9 templates as plain text, and now go through your entire book and format all your main titles to be headings.

You can also save a lot of time if you also pre-format the titles to the font and size you want which will dynamically update each time you make text into Headers.

How to TOC in Pages (Mac)

Insert —> Table of Contents —> Document

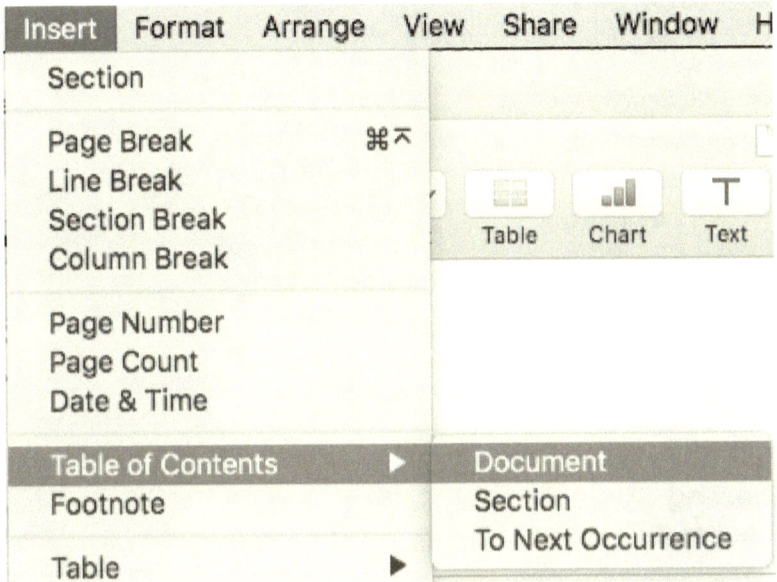

You will see this:

The table of contents is empty because you aren't using the paragraph styles set to appear in it.

Now you can build up your TOC by using titles:

Main Title	1
Subtitle	1
Heading	1
Heading 2	1
Heading 3	1
Main Title Secondary	1
Subtitle Secondary	1
Heading Secondary	1
Heading 2 Secondary	1
Heading 3 Secondary	1

Shows up as....

Main Title

Subtitle

Heading

Heading 2

Heading 3

Main Title Secondary

Subtitle Secondary

Heading Secondary

Heading 2 Secondary

Heading 3 Secondary

You can see that what you write and highlight your text as, shows up in your TOC automatically formatted.

If you decide to change the TOC and you want to only see a few of those titles, just uncheck the TOC boxes of the headers of what you want to show up, on the right:

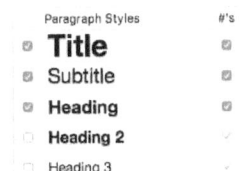

You can see the TOC dynamically change as you do this. It saves you a ton of time because you can also pre-format what the headings should be on the right under Format.

You can also go to the **Text** tab and format the titles so they change to be what you want:

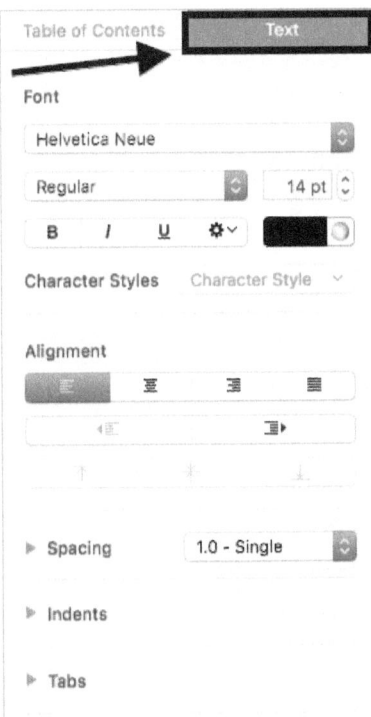

How to TOC on MS Word

You can insert a Table of Contents and then set up the titles to be different headings so that they show up automatically.

Menu —> Insert —> Index and Tables

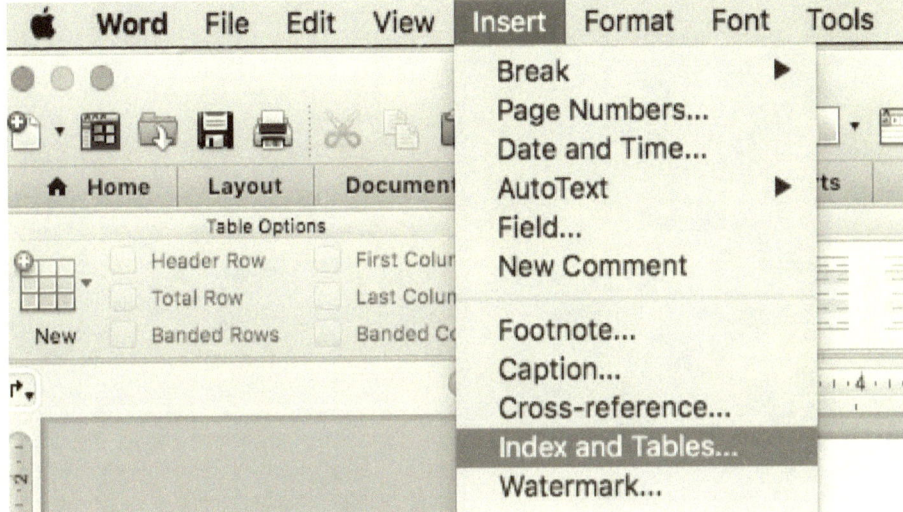

And then you can select the style of TOC:

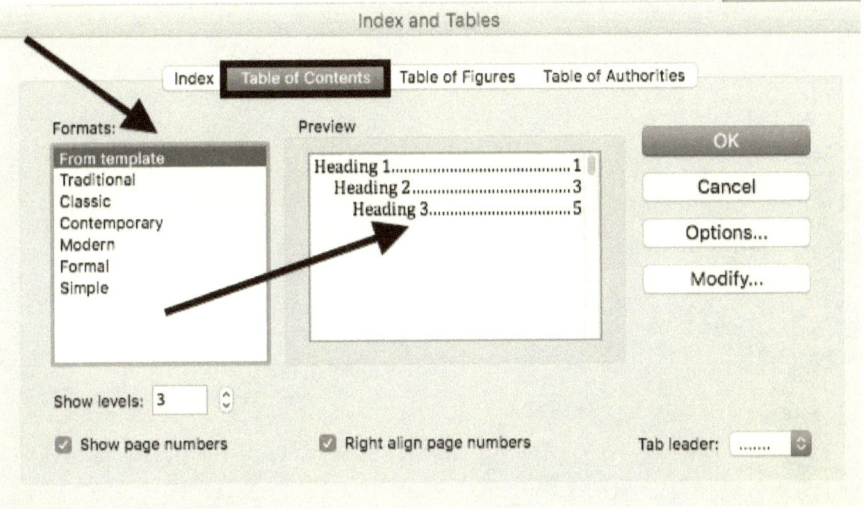

Each of the titles shows you how it would show up if you changed each title to Heading 1, Heading 2 or Heading 3. When you add the TOC, you will see no entries are there yet if you haven't formatted the document with Headings.

Word did not find any entries for your table of contents.

When you go to format the text to become Headings, select the titles and then change it to Heading 1, 2 or 3 under the **Styles** box:

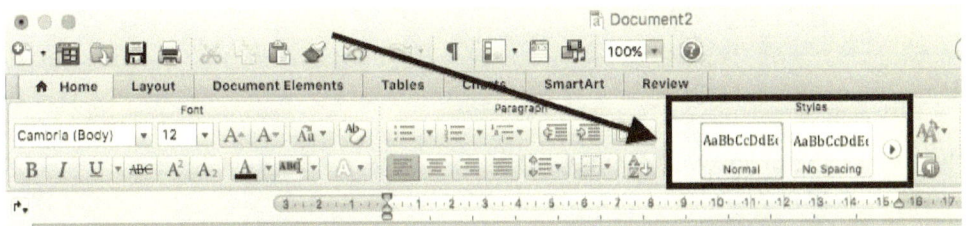

And then click on the arrow NEXT to see the Heading 1, Heading 2 and so on to change it to be a Heading:

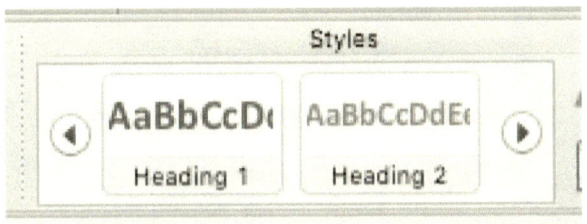

You can also use the menu as **Menu —> Format —> Style**

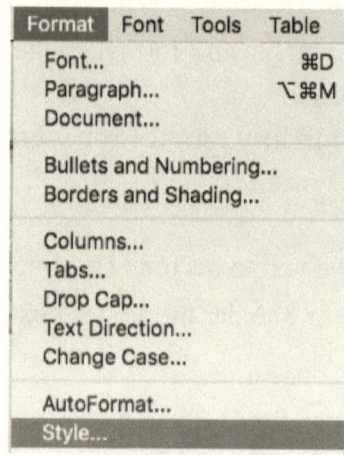

Then you can select what to change the text to:

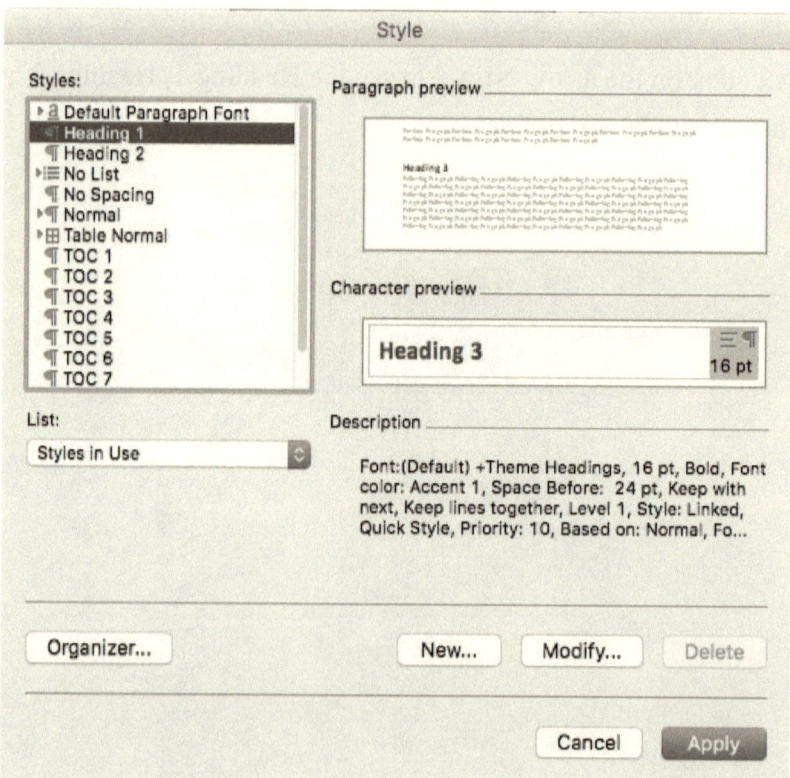

You can also change the font settings in this menu to auto-update to what you want it to be. Select **Modify** and then you can edit the font settings (size, colour, type etc):

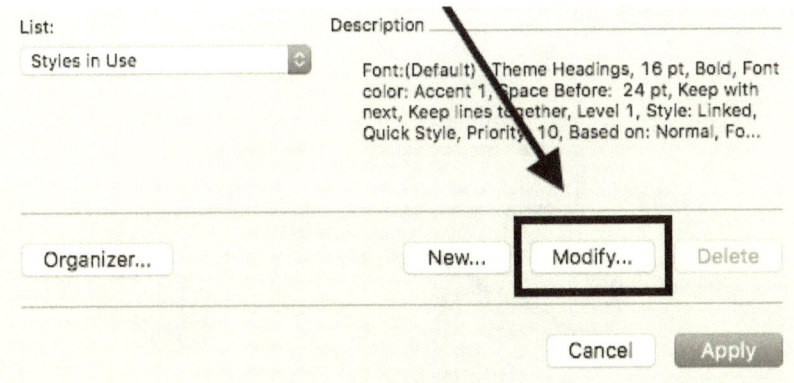

And you have a lot of control here to modify it to be what you want:

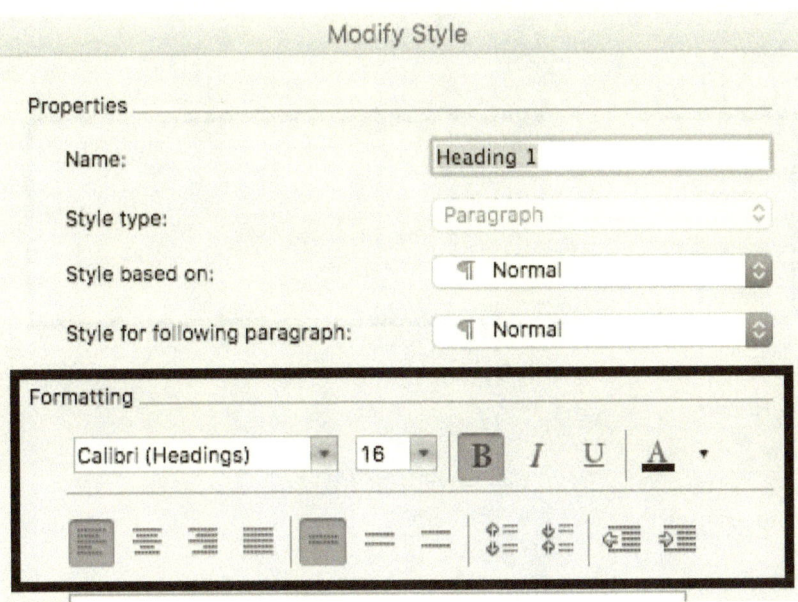

Once you are done formatting the headings, you can right-click on the Table of Contents and update it to refresh:

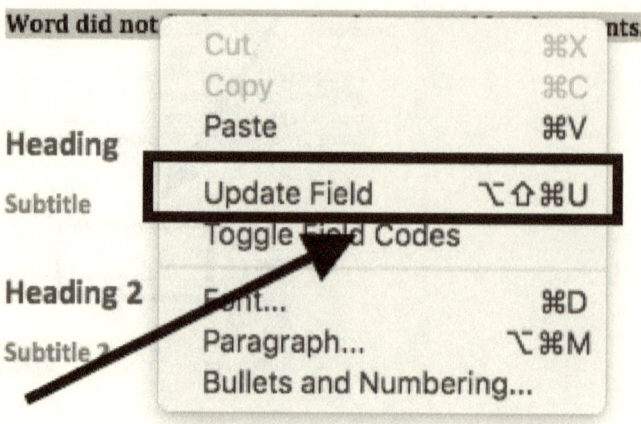

And now you see the TOC at the top updated, and the text below that you formatted:

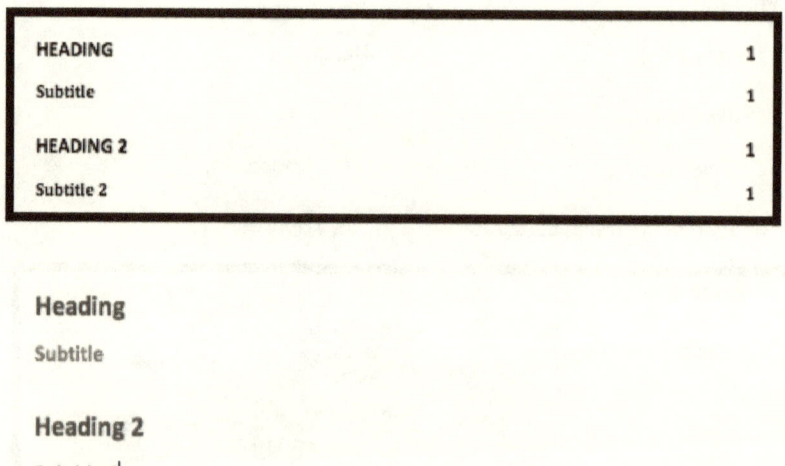

Format Page Break (Pages Mac)

Always make sure you set a page break right after the text as shown below:

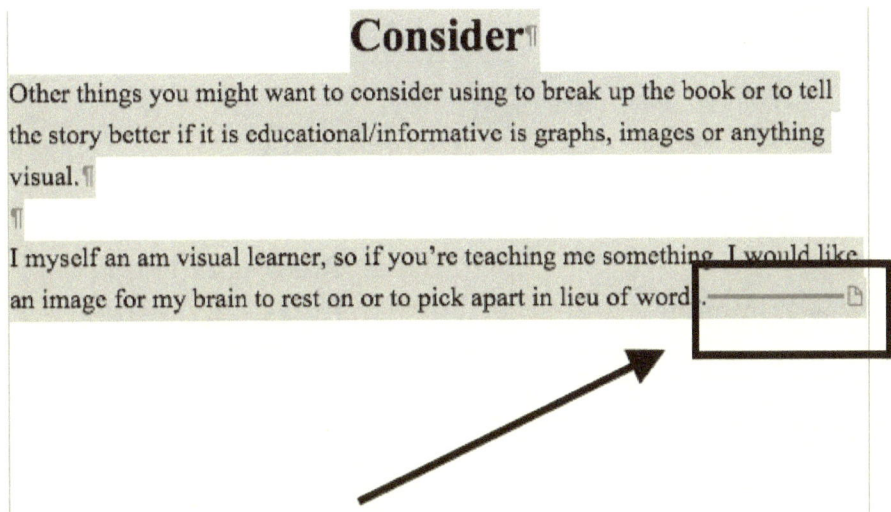

Or close to the image as possible like this:

You want to do this because page breaks are crucial to making sure your book flows properly in e-book format. When people read on ebook readers, they can be reading on anything and with any sizing. They can also choose to make the font bigger to read, smaller, etc.

You really need to pay attention to these page breaks so that you don't end up with awkward blank spots in your page, or sentences cutting off on one page and not flowing well to the next. In Pages (Mac) if you don't see the formatting, you need to highlight the whole text to see all the formatting behind the scenes.

Format Page Break (MS Word)

In MS word to do a page break, it is **Menu —> Insert —> Page Break**

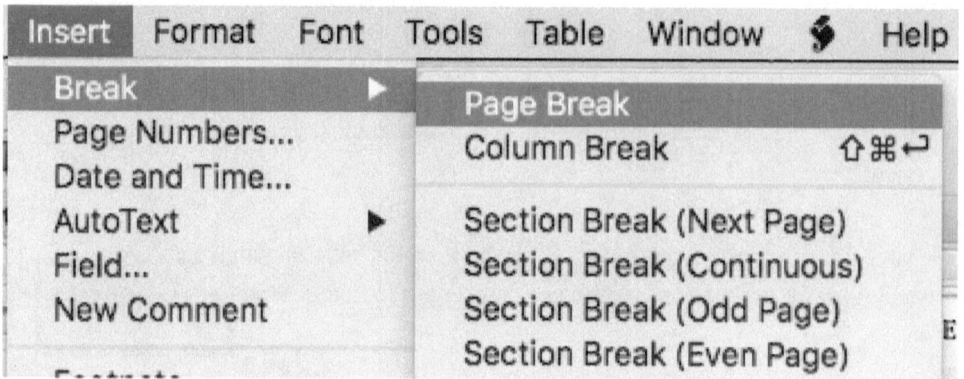

And it will show this:

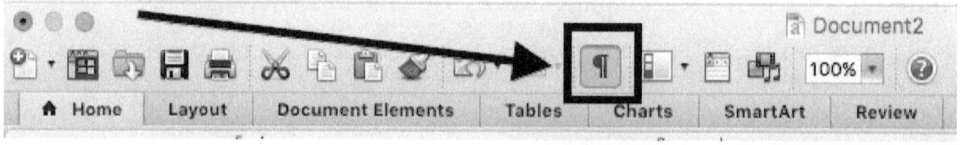

Heading 3

If you don't see this in MS Word, you can click on **Format**:

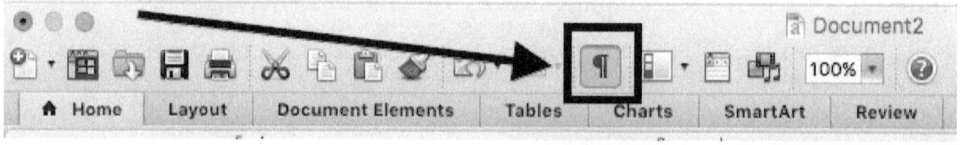

You can also access the formatting view like this: **Menu —> View —> Draft**

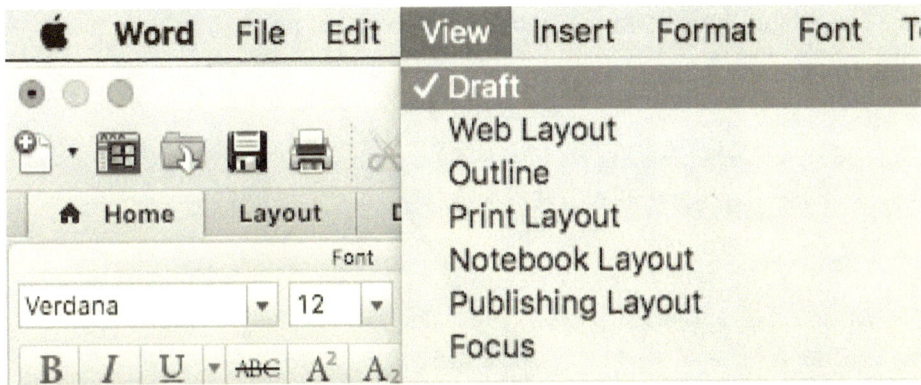

And then you will see all the formatting show up.

If you want to go back to viewing it as if you're reading it, click on **Print Layout**.

Leave a few Spaces on Pages

Leave a few blank lines from the bottom of the actual page:

Consider

Other things you might want to consider using to break up the book or to tell the story better if it is educational/informative is graphs, images or anything visual.

I myself an am visual learner, so if you're teaching me something, I would like an image for my brain to rest on or to pick apart in lieu of words.

Don't write to the very end because as mentioned - people read on different e-readers and in different sizes/formats.

If you write to the end, it can cause an awkward page where a single word gets cut off and pushed to a fully blank page.

Even with images, don't make them go right to the end of the page, and always set a page break just after them (as close as possible) as a marker for ebook readers to know when to break:

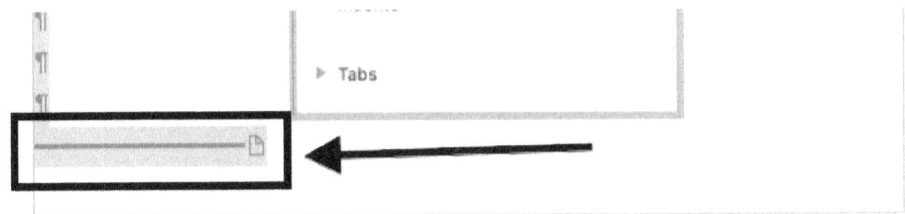

To keep things flowing, always try and leave a few blank lines at the bottom, and/or start another Page Break completely with a thought if it is too much to contain on one page so that it reads and flows better.

At the very least, you will also see in the Preview of the book what it would look like before you publish it, and you can make adjustments then.

Think of your texts

A title is 25% of what sells a book. If it sounds interesting, people are more likely to click on it.

Keep it short - if you make it too long, it won't fit nicely on a cover.

Underneath that main title, is your subtitle. It has to say something specific yet concise about what you are going to talk about. You can add what you wanted to say in the title underneath.

Lastly, your blurb, or description is what people will read to decide whether to spend money on your book or not. It has to grab them in some way.

All of these need to revolve around a core message of what it is you are trying to convey in a book.

Examples of my book titles, and as I am creating a series of informative guides, I always add my tag **Like a Boss**:

- **Start a Blog <u>Like a Boss</u>** - How to make money
- **Managing Money <u>Like a Boss</u>** - The Money Management Picture Book
- **Investing <u>Like a Boss</u>** - Very little work for a big reward
- **Instagram Level Up <u>Like a Boss</u>** - The DIY Guide to Secret Tips & Tricks

Book Cover considerations

You will need a book cover, obviously. It can be difficult to come up with something that is eye-catching yet interesting but not too busy or difficult to deal with.

Consider that you may also write more books (a series?) so if you pick something, can you replicate it or create different variations on it?

That's the thought process that went through my mind when I wrote my first book. I wasn't sure if I was going to create more books, but I wasn't going to make my cover complicated and/or not be able to create a series out of it.

Creating a book cover doesn't have to be difficult. There are great resources with copyright-free for commercial & personal use sites out there that offer stock photos you can use like **Unsplash** (https://www.unsplash.com). More on that later in **PUBLISH**.

The only mandatory thing I would say, is to make sure your background for your cover (if you do a solid colour like mine), takes from one of Amazon's Cover Colours.

Make the image as big as possible so you can use it for a variety of options, with the highest resolution you can, even if it looks massive.

When things go into print, they need to be extra large so that it looks sharp, crisp and clean; what you see on your screen is not the actual size of the original file, it was likely a hundred or a thousand times larger than what is shown.

For instance, my covers for my books are 3780 pixels by 5314 pixels wide, but when you see it on the screen, it only looks like it is 800 pixels wide or so. If I had uploaded a lower resolution image at a smaller size of the 800 pixels you see, the final end product would look very blurry and muddled.

This is called "lost image quality", because as you enlarge a photo, the pixels get enlarged/blurry as well. Think of a nice but small profile picture you have of yourself - have you ever tried to take it out to make it a full-sized page image? It looks terrible because the pixels get stretched out.

More on how to create a cover will be under the section: **PUBLISH**.

Craft your Author Bio

Short little bite of who you are in a nutshell. Keep it short, simple, and if you want, a little light because I personally love authors with a sense of humour. Say something about yourself but not clichéd like enjoying long walks on the beach.

You'll want a nice clear headshot of yourself, with a background that isn't too busy, in proper lighting.

You can do this picture with your cellphone as long as the resolution is decent, and try out different looks:

- with or without glasses if you wear any
- hair up or down
- a few different shirts/jackets (you're taking a shoulders-up photo)
- Smiling and not smiling (with or without teeth)

Then send your top 3 pictures to a bunch of honest, impartial friends, and ask them to vote. You can send them in a few rounds such as pictures with you smiling but with different shirts/jackets on, and then whichever ones looked best, take only those pictures with the best shirt/jacket combination, and send your smiling, unsmiling, glasses/no glasses photos to narrow it down.

Then do another final round of photos to make sure you've chosen the best one. The one people in general like the most, is your best one, even if you think it isn't flattering as **you can't really look at yourself objectively**.

If you're Anonymous like I am, try sunglasses, or a large sunhat, or a silhouette. You can still show yourself without showing your face.

PUBLISH

Amazon Help

If you want lots of technical, dry answers to specific questions, Amazon Help is great. I won't be reposting all of what they have on their site here.

You can read it yourself:
https://kdp.amazon.com/en_US/help/topic/G200635650

They have a lot of specific answers to a lot of questions that you may have.

A lot of what Amazon posts is very technical, and it might take you some time to read through it (I had to DIY educate myself), so a good rule of thumb is to try not to customize everything and keep it simple.

The more complications you add such as trying to become too fancy, will cause your workload to increase if you have never published a book before.

Keep it simple for the first one, and then for subsequent books once you're more comfortable, you can kick it up a notch.

This guide already helps you do the basics of that, setting the correct trim size, and how to do a cover, and once you feel like you can do more, then add more and go for it!

Don't try to print on your own

When I first printed my book - **Start a Blog like a Boss** I thought I would print it all on my own and it'd be cheaper.

WRONG.

It's cheaper to get a big company that does this all the time, to print it for you. The costs you will pay depending on how many pages you have, will be worth the lack of headache and hassle, which is why I recommend Amazon Publishing so strongly.

They have the cost-effective means, methods and distribution to have your book printed, mailed and sold in an ebook format to go worldwide, and even end up in libraries or stores if there is a demand (this is called **Expanded distribution**).

Printing it on your own is a waste of time, a headache and not worth it at all.

Plus, where are you going to store all of these books that you've ordered in print, to ship out!?

I still have the 2 large printed books I printed from my original blunder, sitting in my closet as a reminder.

Use a common trim size

The best way to publish a book on the cheap (so you don't bleed out on printing costs), and to make sure it is accessible to the masses is to use a cheap and cheerful template and book size. They call this the **Trim Size.**

Here are the options they give you and it is overwhelming:

Trim size	Black ink and white paper	Black ink and cream paper	Color ink and white paper
5" x 8" (12.7 x 20.32 cm)	24 - 828	24 - 776	24 - 828
5.06" x 7.81" (12.85 x 19.84 cm)	24 - 828	24 - 776	24 - 828
5.25" x 8" (13.34 x 20.32 cm)	24 - 828	24 - 776	24 - 828
5.5" x 8.5" (13.97 x 21.59 cm)	24 - 828	24 - 776	24 - 828
6" x 9" (15.24 x 22.86 cm)	24 - 828	24 - 776	24 - 828
6.14" x 9.21" (15.6 x 23.39 cm)	24 - 828	24 - 776	24 - 828
6.69" x 9.61" (16.99 x 24.41 cm)	24 - 828	24 - 776	24 - 828
7" x 10" x (17.78 x 25.4 cm)	24 - 828	24 - 776	24 - 828
7.44" x 9.69" (18.9 x 24.61 cm)	24 - 828	24 - 776	24 - 828
7.5" x 9.25" (19.05 x 23.5 cm)	24 - 828	24 - 776	24 - 828
8" x 10" (20.32 x 25.4 cm)	24 - 828	24 - 776	24 - 828
8.25" x 6" (20.96 x 15.24 cm)	24 - 800	24 - 750	24 - 800
8.25" x 8.25" (20.96 x 20.96 cm)	24 - 800	24 - 750	24 - 800
8.5" x 8.5" (21.59 x 21.59 cm)	24 - 590	24 - 550	24 - 590
8.5" x 11" (21.59 x 27.94 cm)	24 - 590	24 - 550	24 - 590
8.27" x 11.69" (21 x 29.7 cm)	24 - 780	24 - 730	Not available

I've tried doing larger books, smaller books, and the best format is **Paperback** which is 6" x 9". **Paperback** is the most common size to print books in, and it doesn't require a special printing press or any extra modifications.

It is so easy to print and read in an eBook format (remember, people can size it to what they wish), and doesn't cost a fortune to ship (you're paying for that too, indirectly, especially since Amazon offers free shipping).

When I first printed my book - **Start a Blog like a Boss** - I had way more technical screenshots, and full-length pages that I thought I needed a large 11.69" x 6.27" book that would make sense.

It was almost a custom-printed book each time because no one printed a book that size!!!

From the printing costs alone, I was unable to break even until I sold the third book. It was NOT a good idea, so I reformatted the whole book to be a smaller template that was easily printed.

You can use the pre-formatted 6" x 9" templates I have provided with this book for the Mac and MS Word so you don't need to fret about trim size or margins.

Set your Document Trim Sizes

You need to set a custom size in either Pages (Mac) or MS Word so that the document is 6" x 9" for instance.

To do this in Pages (Mac):

Go to **Menu** —> **File** —> **Page Setup**

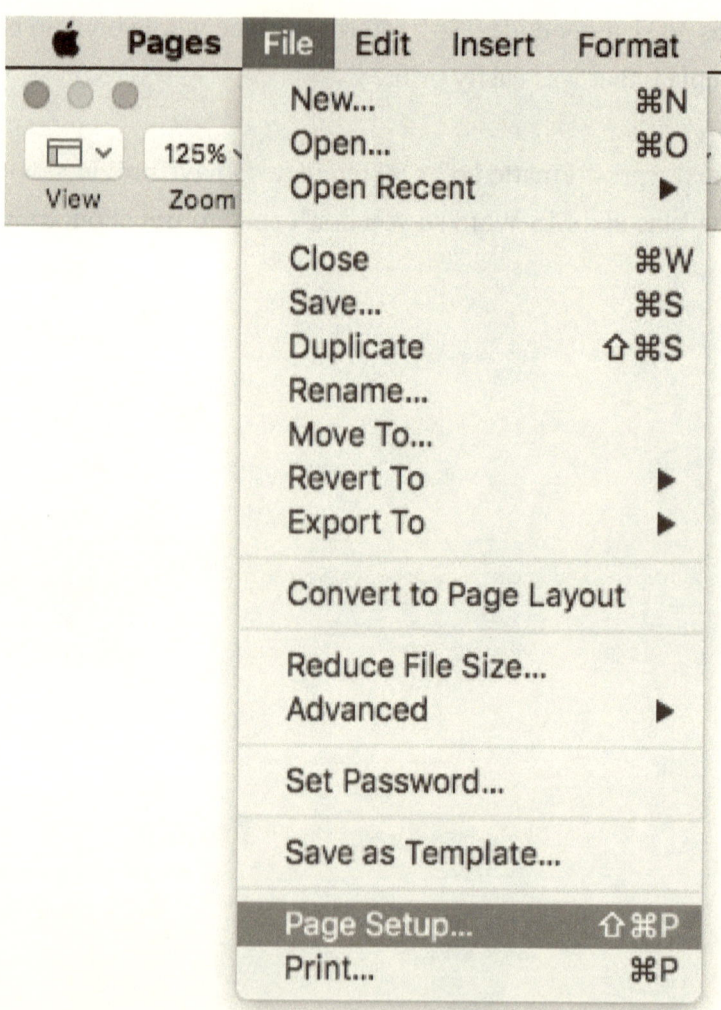

Under **Paper Size**

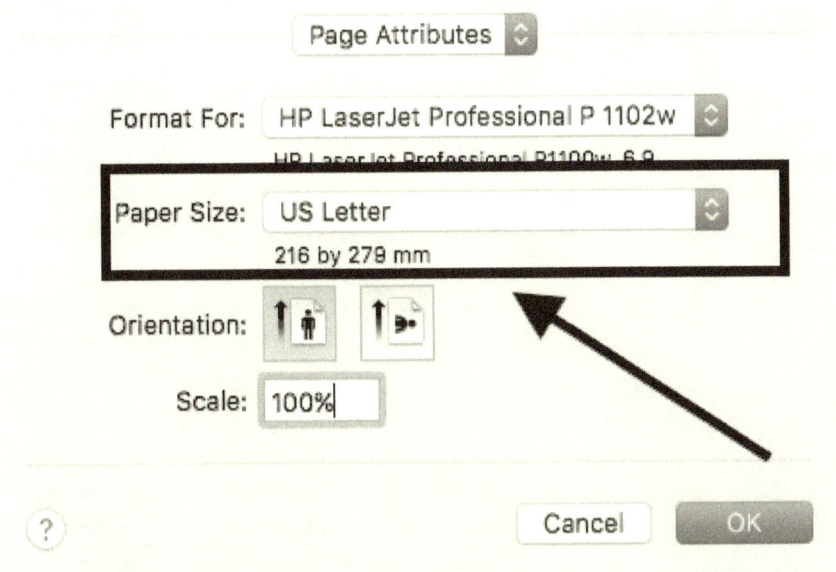

Select **Manage Custom Sizes**

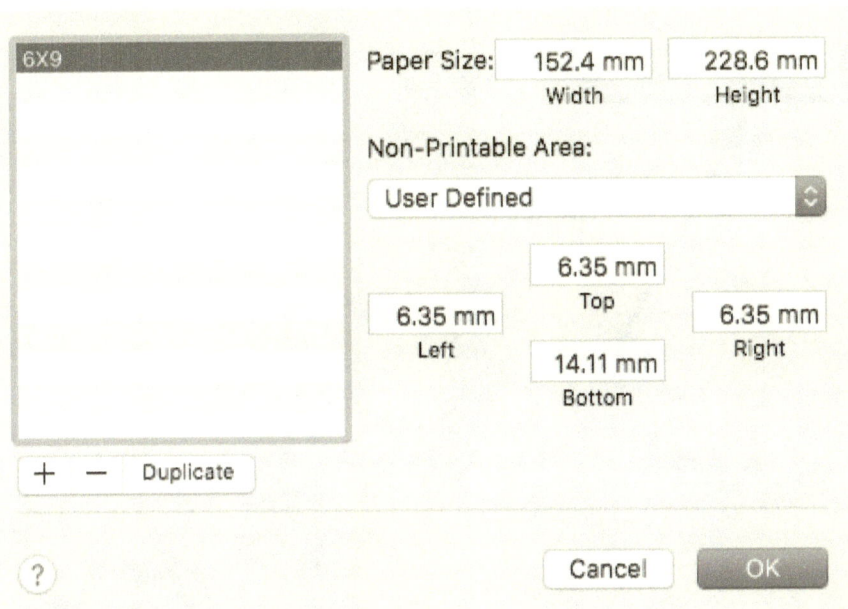

Click on the + button at the bottom left to add a new custom size:

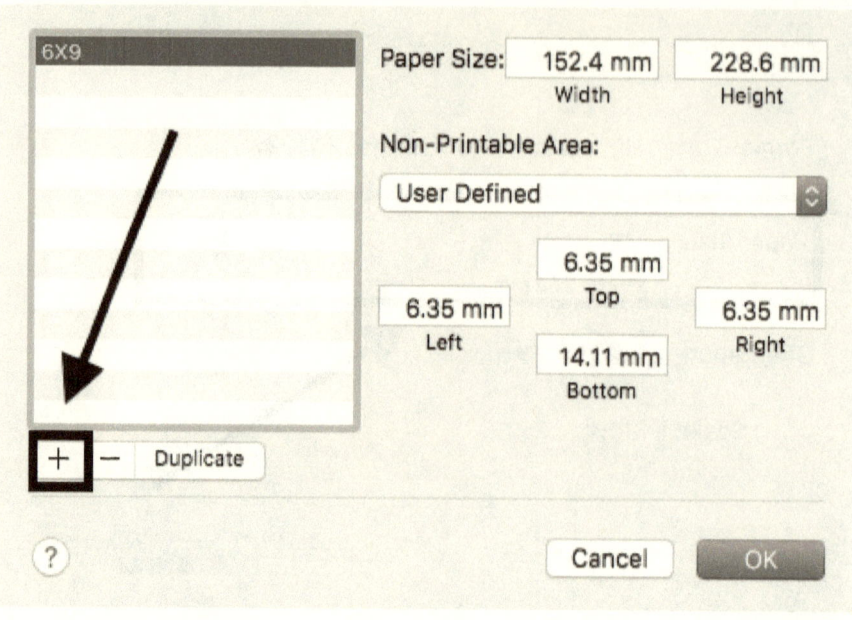

Tap on the name **Untitled** to rename it to **6X9** or whatever you want it to be:

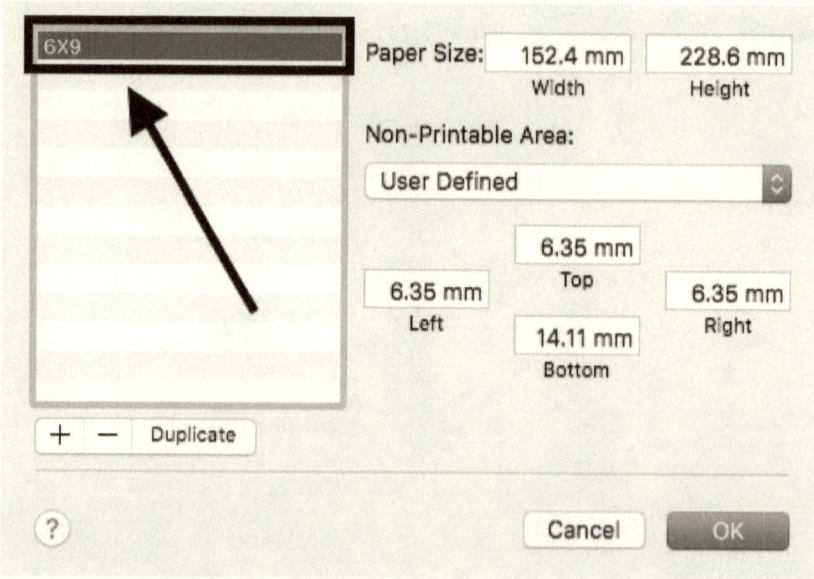

Change the size to these dimensions for 6" x 9":

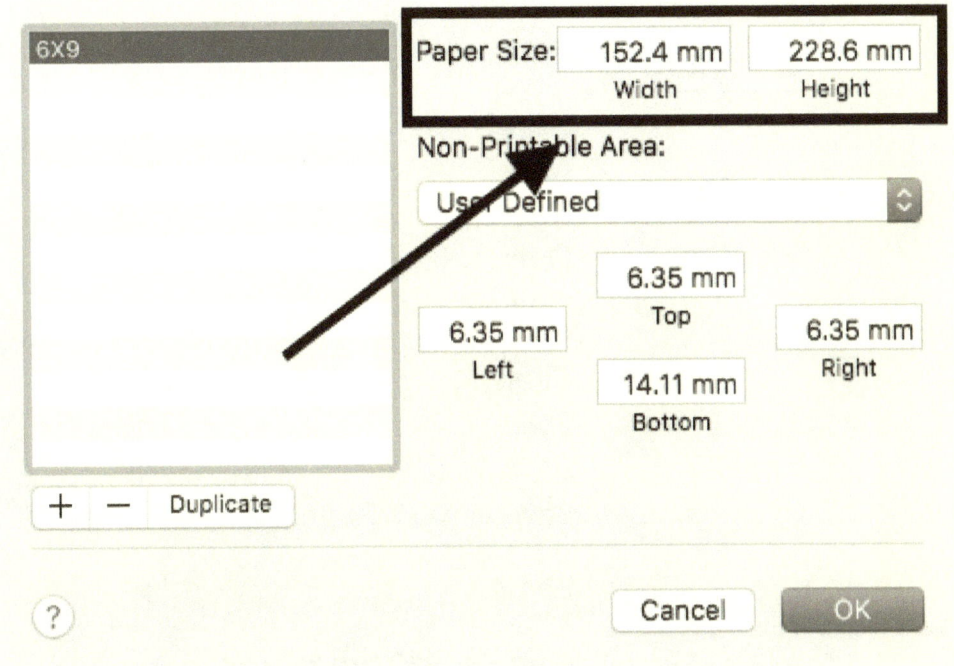

Click **OK** to save.

To do this in MS Word:

Go to **Menu —> File —> Page Setup**

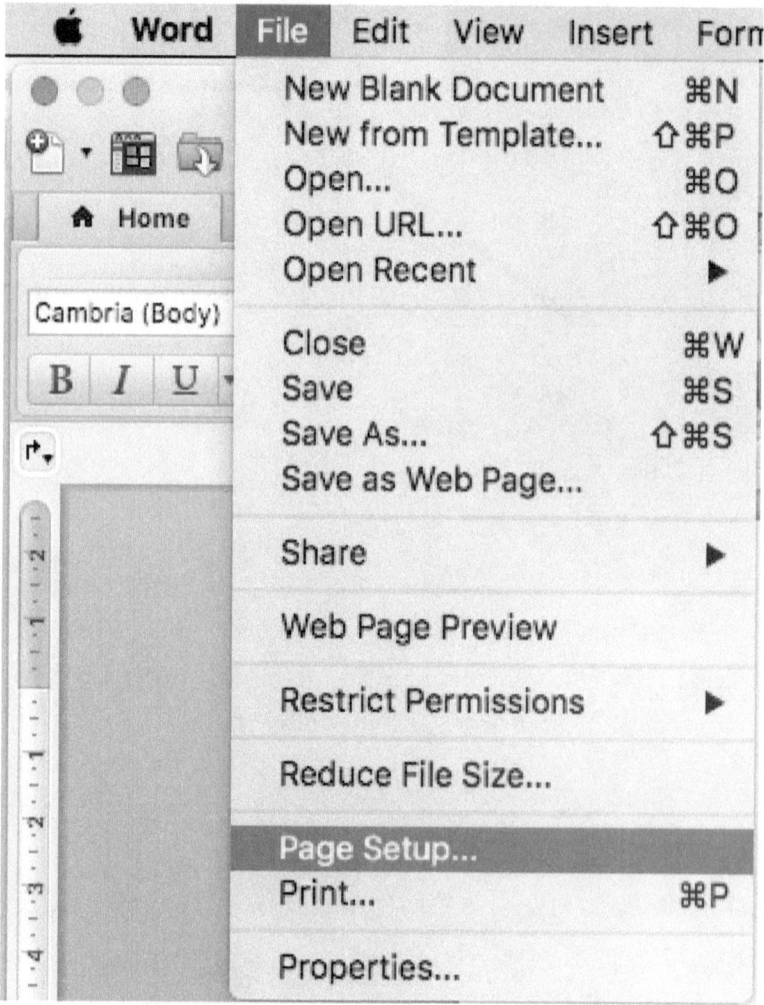

Under **Paper Size**

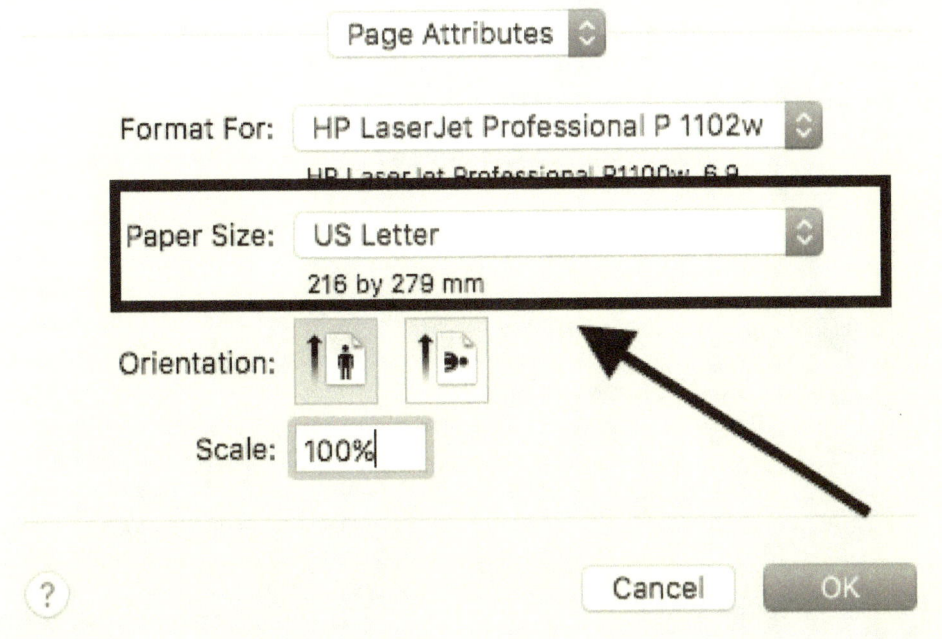

Select **Manage Custom Sizes**

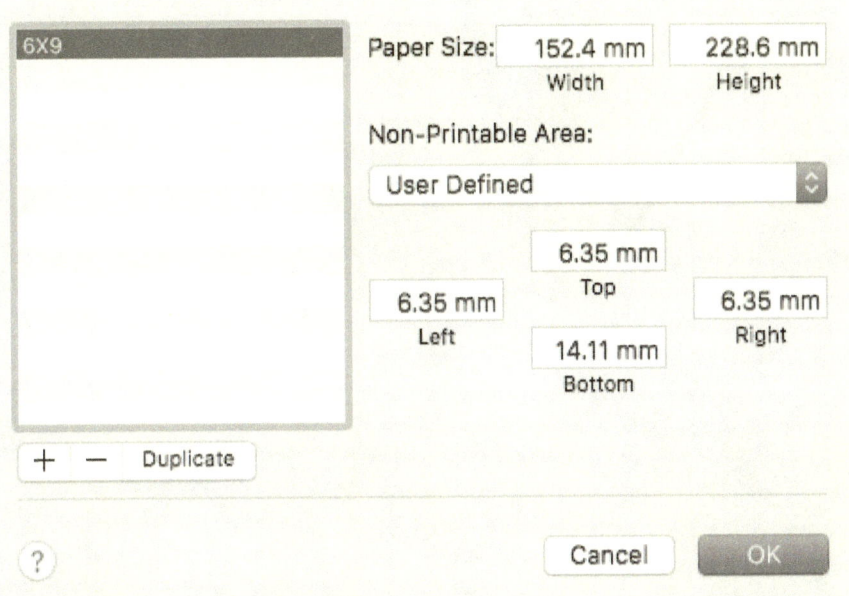

Click on the + button at the bottom left to add a new custom size:

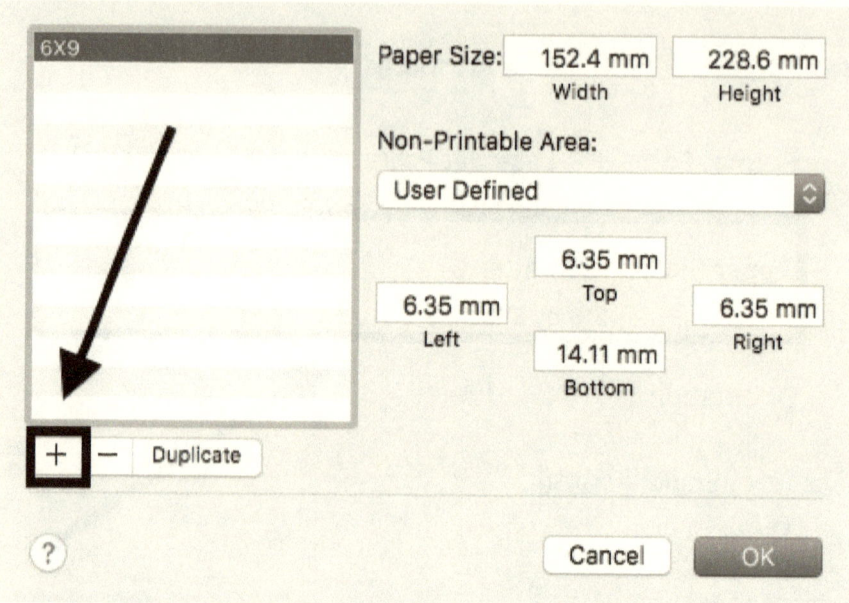

Tap on the name **Untitled** to rename it to **6X9** or whatever you want it to be:

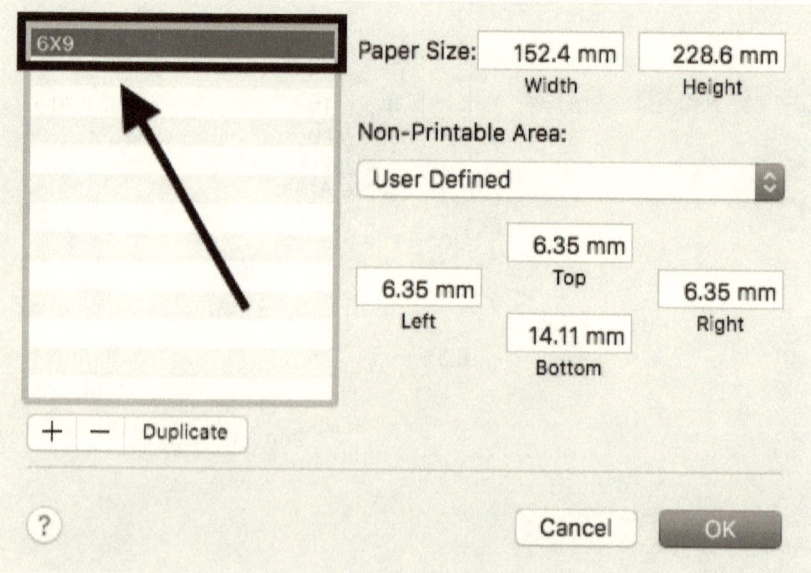

Change the size to these dimensions for 6" x 9":

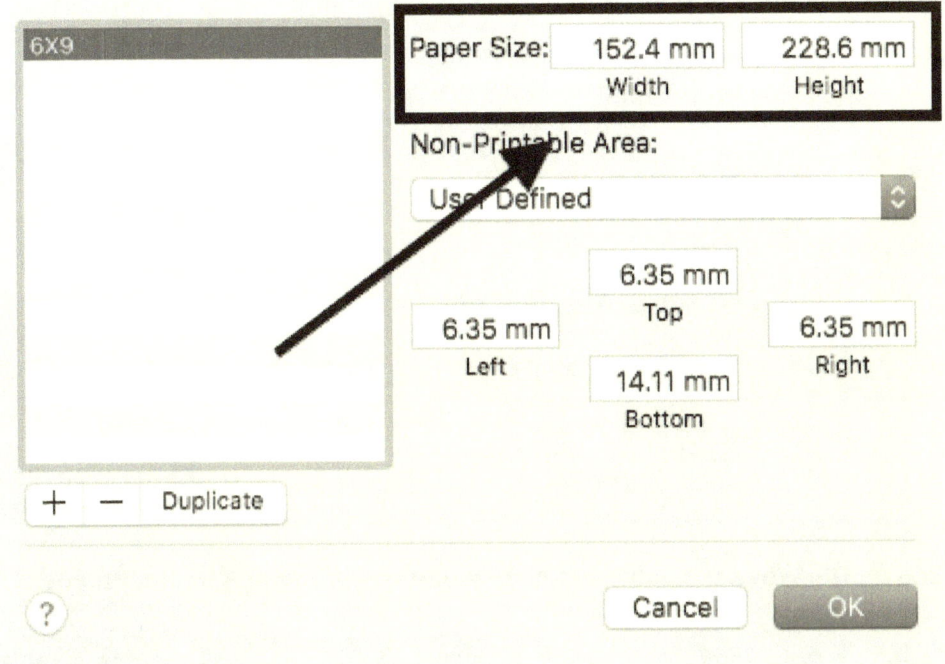

Click **OK** to save.

Set your trim size for your books

Before you copy & paste or type, now you can simply go into **Pages** (**Mac**) under **Document** and select your custom trim size you created in the upper right corner of your document:

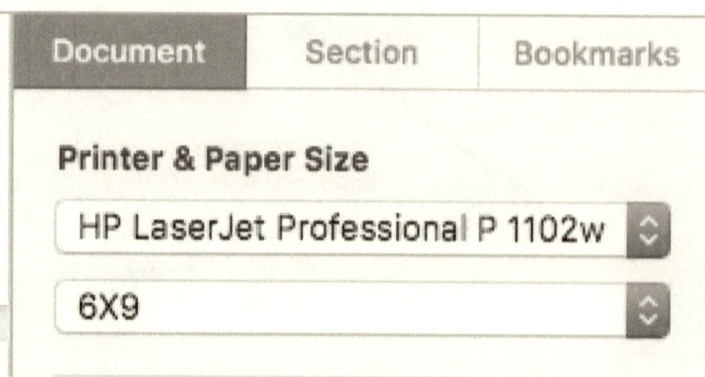

And in **MS Word** it can be set under **Menu** —> **Format** —> **Document**:

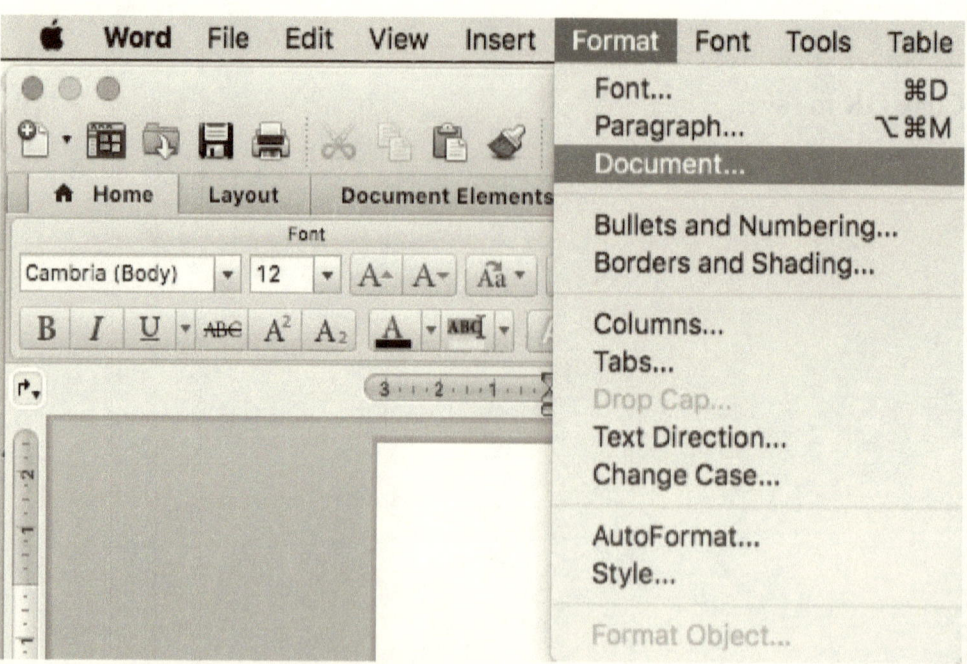

Click on **Page Setup** at the bottom:

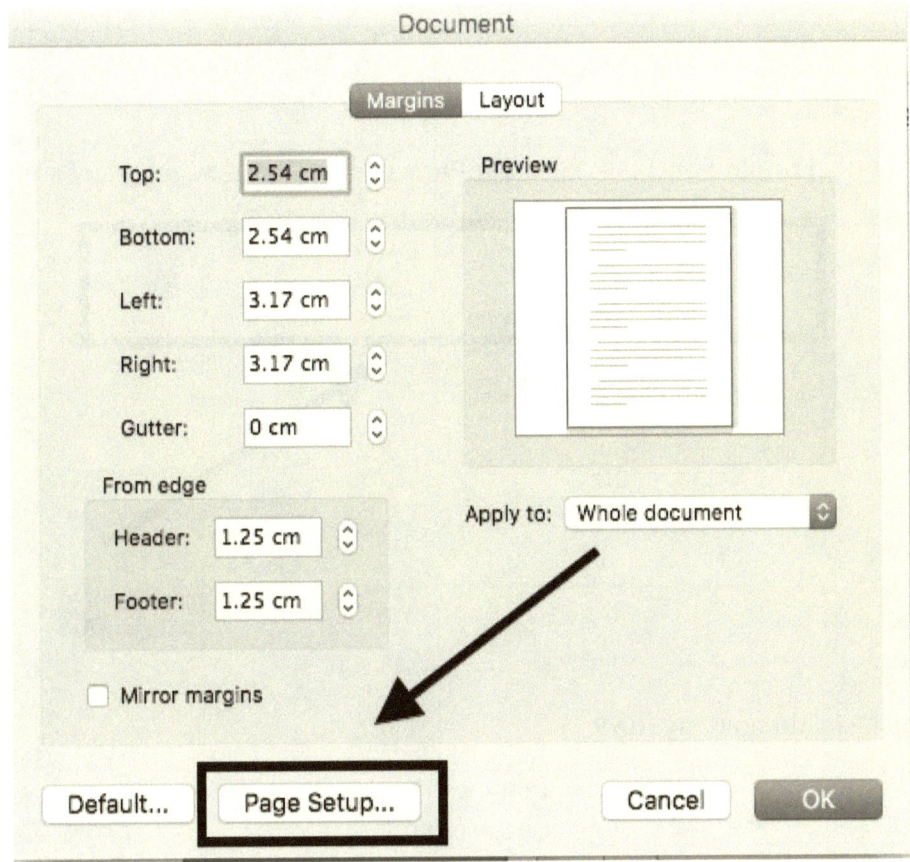

And under **Paper Size**, select your custom Trim Size you created:

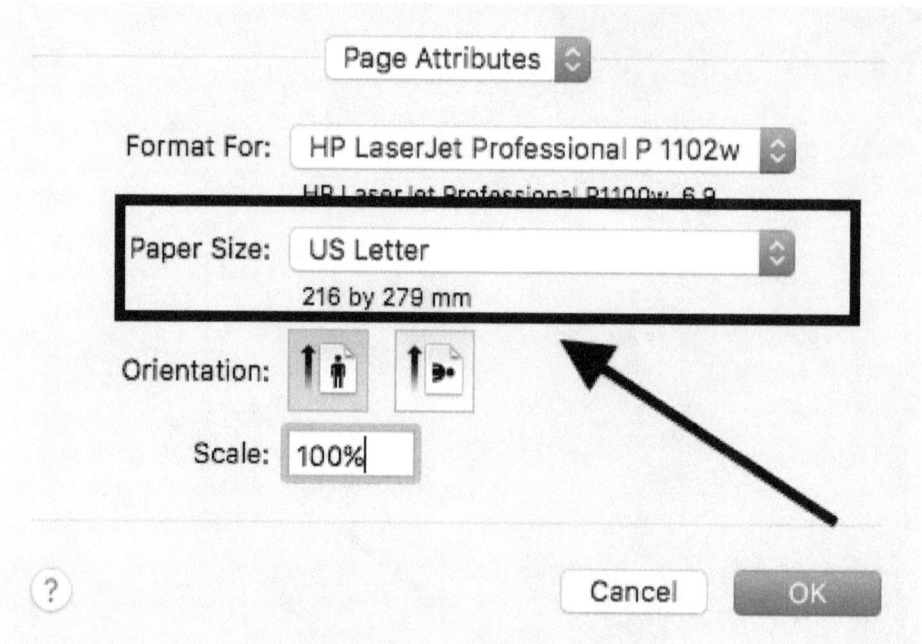

Which should now say: **6X9**

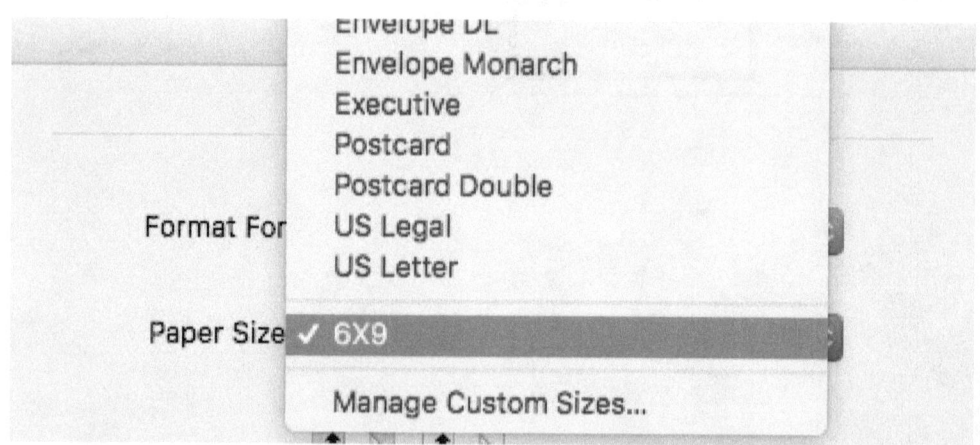

Click **OK**, then **OK** again and you're done.

How to change your margins

You'll can play around with the margins to adjust it so that as you're typing your text, so it doesn't look too close to the edge, or too 'tight' when you're reading.

In Pages (Mac), you can set the margins here under **Document** —> **Document Margins** especially if your book is very thick & needs extra inner margins to print & be read properly.

To do this in MS Word, you have to go from **Menu —> Format —> Document**

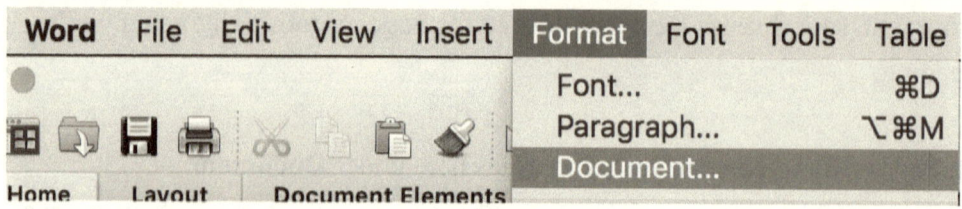

You can change the margins here and apply it.

Create a Publisher Account

Now that your book is properly formatted, the margins are good, you can start the actual publishing process on Amazon.

Create an account here, on Kindle Direct Publishing (KDP) (https://kdp.amazon.com/). You can link it to your personal Amazon account, or create a whole new, separate Amazon account with another email address and start anew.

Sign in with your Amazon login

If you are new to KDP, you can use an Amazon login to register. Just sign in with your existing Amazon login or create a new account.

I decided to separate my personal Amazon account from my blog one, so I have one created just for my blog that I handle all my business and books under.

It might be a good idea to separate them - you never know if one day you might want to, and if you intertwine them from the start, it could be hard to separate afterwards.

Setup Kindle eBook details

You will get two options when you want to start your book.

I suggest doing the ebook option first, and then the printed one afterwards, as the printed one takes more time to modify and setup.

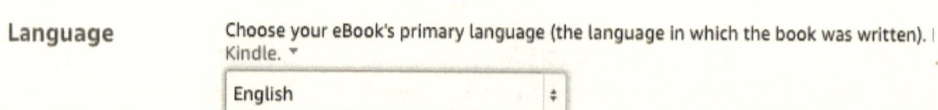

Create a New Title

+
Kindle eBook

Book Content: You can upload a manuscript, or use our free creation tools to create children's books, educational content, comics, and manga. Get started with Kindle content creation tools.

Book Cover: You can use our online Cover Creator, or upload a cover of your own. Creating a great cover.

Description, Keywords and Categories: Tell readers about your book and help them find it on Amazon.

+
Paperback

ISBN: Get a free ISBN to publish your paperback. Kindle eBooks don't need one. More about ISBNs.

See all Getting Started tips ›

LANGUAGE

Straightforward - choose the language your book is in.

Amazon supports a lot of languages on the Kindle, and in Preview you can

Language   Choose your eBook's primary language (the language in which the book was written). I
            Kindle. ▾

            English   ⬍

see if it shows up correctly or not.

BOOK TITLE & SUBTITLE

Type in your actual book title.

This is important that you type it in exactly as you want to see it in eBook and Print as you cannot modify it to say differently when you go to do your book covers - Amazon will tell you that it is a mismatch and you will have a headache if your title doesn't match what you actually want it to say.

Book Title   Enter your title as it will appear on the book cover.

Book Title

Publish a Book Like a Boss

Subtitle (Optional)

The Fast Guide to Selling on Amazon

SERIES

If you're creating a series, you can certainly type it in here, but this is optional.

Series   The series name and volume number will help customers find other books in your series on Amazon.

Series Information (Optional)

Like a Boss   5

EDITION NUMBER

Also optional but if you plan on doing extra updated versions, it can help previous buyers know that this is a new and revised version #2 or #3.

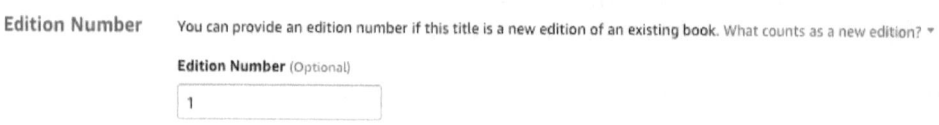

AUTHOR

You must put a last name. You can just put an initial like I have.

This will also show up as your author name and clickable link in the bio when your book publishes:

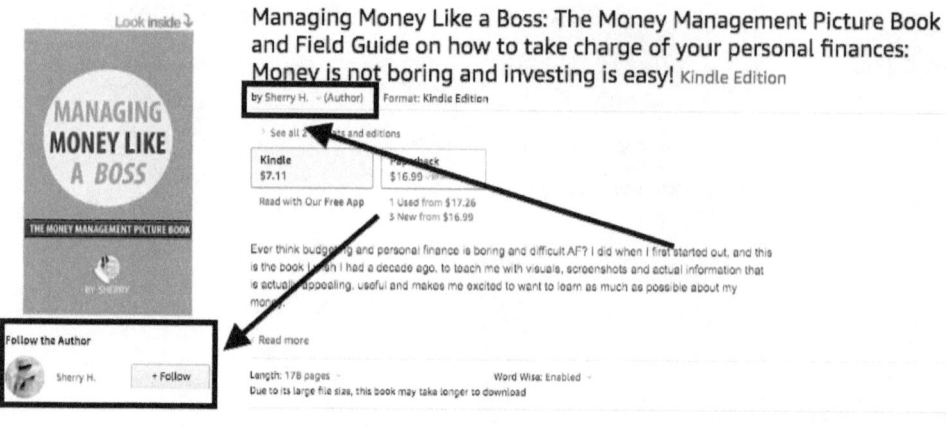

DESCRIPTION

Description   This will appear on your book's Amazon detail page. Why do book descriptions matter? ˅

Want to become a published author within a day?

Assuming your content is written, it's quite easy to become published if you have the templates and the ins-and-outs of what to

3308
characters left

Your book description is CRUCIAL. Spend the MOST time on here, please.

The first paragraph is what shows up in your listing for the book, so make them impactful and the potential buyer interested in clicking to read more:

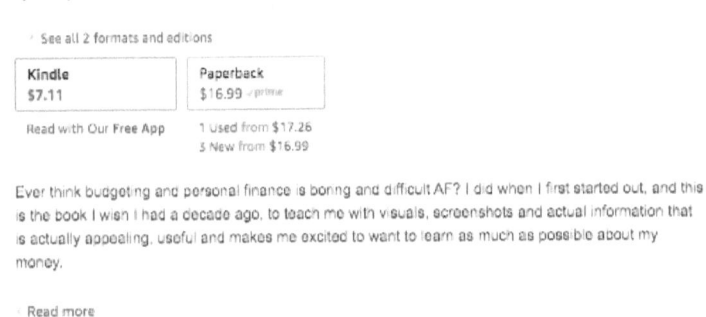

See this listing for my book above? You will see the first paragraph, but if you're interested, you'd click **Read more**.

Make people want to click **Read more**. Keep it simple, short, and engaging. Then, when they click **Rad more**, you can add as much information as you want, maybe a Table of Contents, etc.

PUBLISHING RIGHTS

| Publishing Rights | ⦿ I own the copyright and I hold the necessary publishing rights. What are publishing rights? ▾ |
| | ○ This is a public domain work. What is a public domain work? ▾ |

If you have written the book - it's your work.

KEYWORDS

This says optional but it really isn't.

The more keywords you have that are not your title, that add more description and are adjacent to what your book is about, the better chance you have of when people search for similar books and find yours.

| Keywords | Enter up to 7 search keywords that describe your book. To enter the Kindle Storyteller contest, you need to add the keyword StorytellerUK2020. How do I choose keywords? ▾ |

Your Keywords (Optional)

Guide to Publish on Amazon	DIY Author Help for Amazon
Help for Authors to Publish	Side Income Hustle
Publishing Books FAQ	Make Money Fast
Selling a Book on Amazon	

Think about what your reader will get out of it - be creative!

Don't think about what your book literally talks about, think about what would entice someone who is looking for something similar, to come across your book and think: ***That's what I was looking for but didn't know it!***

CATEGORIES

AGE AND GRADE RANGE

This is optional and very useful if you are selling books marketed towards a certain age or grade range. If not, leave them blank.

If you have restricted content (not PG-13), please disclose that.

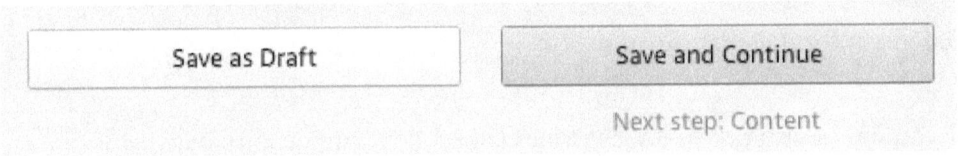

Now you can **Save as Draft** and take a break, or **Save and Continue** and move on to Content (manuscript uploading and cover creation).

Save as Draft	Save and Continue
	Next step: Content

Setup Kindle eBook Content

MANUSCRIPT

It is happening! You're about to upload your document!

Decide what you want to do with DRM (Digital Rights Management).

Manuscript   Please read our KDP Content Guidelines and upload a manuscript containing interior content for your Kindle eBook. View
              supported file types ▾

              Digital Rights Management (DRM)
              Enable DRM on this Kindle eBook. How is my Kindle eBook affected by DRM? ▾

              ○ Yes

              ○ No

Do you want to make sure they can share the book once they buy it and just email it to anyone they want? Or allow the book to be just lent out for a short period of time?

Now you need to upload your eBook manuscript but you have to upload it in certain formats.

Upload eBook manuscript

If you did all of your work in MS word, you're fine - it supports .doc and .docx formats to upload it as-is.

If you did your work in Pages (Mac) (like I do), you need to convert it to ePub first which is very simple. ePub is the standard publishing format for all ebooks, which means it works on Kindles, Kobos, and other e-readers.

How to convert your book to ePub

I would choose ePub conversion over the other formats like Word because it keeps the most accurate formatting of your book, whereas I find MS Word and Pages don't really play nicely with each other at times.

In Pages, click on **Menu —> File —> Export to —> EPUB**

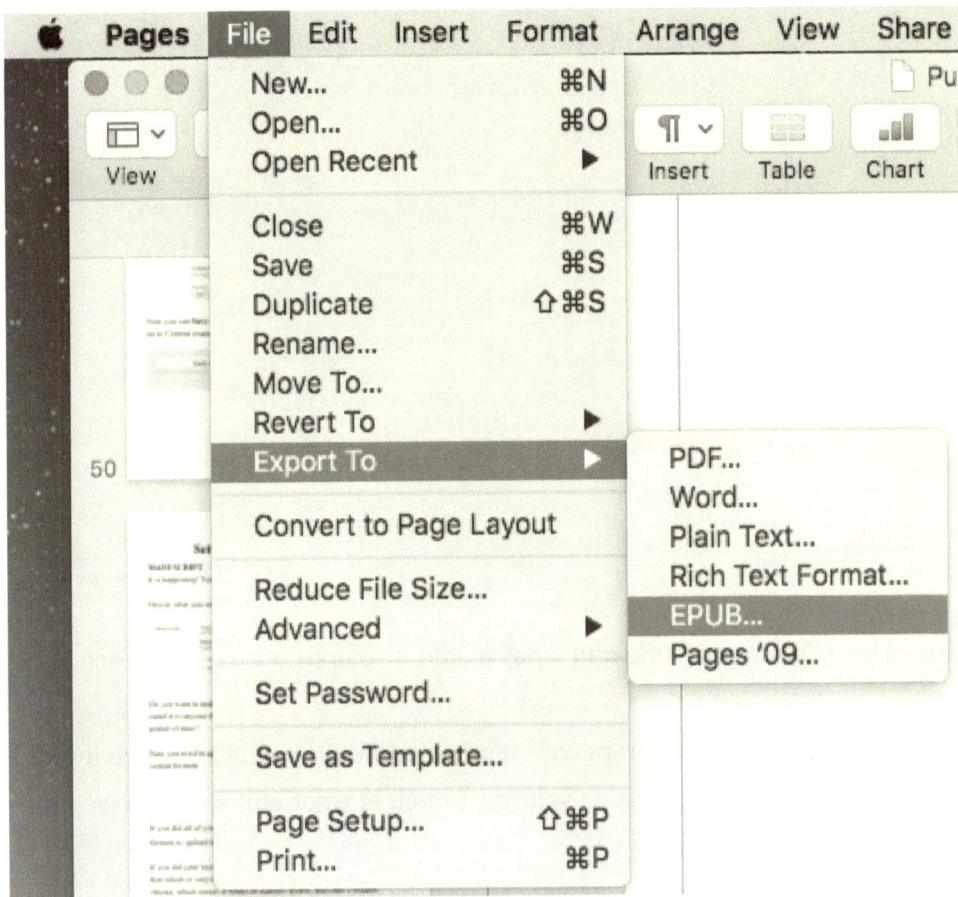

A little window will pop up to ask you how you want to create the EPUB, here's a rundown of what each section means:

Export Your Document

| PDF | Word | Plain Text | RTF | EPUB | Pages '09 |

Title Publish a Book Like a Boss

Author Sherry of Save. Spend. Splurge.

Cover ● No book cover
○ Use the first page as the book cover image
○ Choose an image

Layout ○ Reflowable   ● Fixed layout
The layout of each page in your document will be maintained. Best for image–heavy or multi–column documents.

▼ Advanced Options

Category Teaching & Learning

Language English

View As ● Single Page   ○ Two Pages
☑ Embed Fonts

(?)   Cancel   Next...

Title: This is your book title and what would also appear on an e-reader

Author: This takes your computer's name by default, you can change it like I have, to Sherry of Save. Spend. Splurge. which is what will show up as your author name in an e-reader.

Cover: Set NO book cover for this ePub creation, as you will upload a cover in the next section, otherwise you will end up with two covers for your book.

If you plan on selling this book separately outside of Amazon (like I do), then you want to create a second ePub version that has a cover image so that it looks like the one on the left with your cool cover and not on the right (generic, grey, boring).

I would highly recommend that for your ePub (non-Amazon) version with the cover, to put it in the first page and to use that option rather than trying to upload an image (it won't always work and you may get frustrated trying to figure it out).

Layout: If your book is mostly text, choose **Reflowable**. If your books are mostly image-heavy like mine, choose **Fixed Layout**.

Category: Pick one, it is just for an ereader's classification when a user wants to look at all "Reference books", and so on. Doesn't matter as much.

Before you save the file, I suggest naming it with **EPUB NO COVER** at the end so that you know what format you can easily see in your files what version or layout of the ePub you have in your file name.

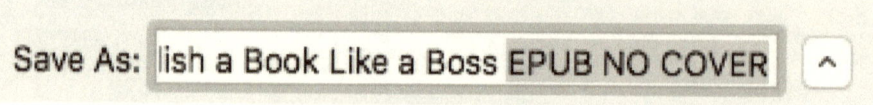

And now you're ready to take this, and upload it onto Amazon.

Setup Kindle eBook Cover

You should get this message before you move on to the cover (Amazon doesn't like it if you skip steps, they get very salty):

> ✓ Manuscript "*Publish a Book Like a Boss EPUB.epub*" uploaded successfully!
> Processing your file...

There are lots of ways you can create and upload a cover from making your own to using Amazon's creator, to choosing images.

The easiest method by far is to have the front cover designed with the colours of Amazon's palette.

See more under **TOOLS - Create a Book Cover in Amazon** on how to create a good Amazon cover and in the colours required for the background.

You only need the first cover for this to shortcut method, but I will go into some other options if you're interested.

They give you two options to create your cover, you can use their **Cover Creator** or you can **Upload your own Cover**

For eBook creation, you want to simply **Upload that cover file** you created.

For print, you will want to use **Cover Creator**. More on that in the next part when we set up your printed book. For now, let's finish the eBook.

Preview your book

You're almost done. Launch Previewer and make sure your formatting with spaces at the end of pages, page breaks and other notes I made above, are tight:

They give you other options to preview the book as well on the main page, but let's use the Previewer. At the top they will show you font size, and what device you are using:

I'd look at it both in **Tablet** and **Kindle E-Reader** mode. Don't fret if things don't look perfect in one or the other - remember that that's what you put in page breaks and spaces at the end of pages, so that it would generally fit all formats.

You can't make it perfect - it is a rabbit hole in trying to achieve that perfection. Remember that people can also zoom in and out, change font sizes - all of this would 'ruin' any perfect layout you could imagine.

What you are checking for here, is simply that words look correct, the pages are not cut off. If you think you can shorten the paragraph/make it more concise - by all means, take the time to edit your manuscript, re-upload it and try again.

I can see for instance, the margins to the right are slightly cut off:

I'd go back to my manuscript and adjust the margins to the right to make sure it fits and my words are not chopped off. If you have done proper page breaks and formatting, this won't affect the manuscript as much in terms of flow.

Once all that is fixed, you're ready to go!

Now click Save & Continue and set your pricing:

Save as Draft	Save and Continue
	Next step: Pricing

ISBN Numbers

ISBN numbers are a unique way to identify your book.

ISBN numbers are not necessary for eBooks, but they can be free and assigned automatically for the print version via Amazon.

The only caveat with Amazon ISBN numbers is you can only use them with Amazon and their partner's publishing system.

If you go with another publisher, you will need a new ISBN number.

Setup Kindle eBook Pricing

KDP SELECT ENROLLMENT

KDP Select Enrollment

Maximize My Royalties with KDP Select (Optional)

With KDP Select, you can reach more readers, earn more money, and maximize your sales potential. To enter the Kindle Storyteller contest, your eBook needs to be enrolled in KDP Select. Learn more about KDP Select. How Do I Enroll? ▾

Visit the Promotions Page to manage your KDP Select Enrollment

They have Amazon KDP Select promotions on and off - read into them and take advantage if it makes sense.

I am personally not enrolled in this particular one, but it would be a good idea if you're a storyteller.

TERRITORIES

Territories

Select the territories for which you hold distribution rights. To enter the Kindle Storyteller contest, you need make your book available at least in Amazon.co.uk. Learn more about distribution rights.

◉ **All territories (worldwide rights)** What are worldwide rights? ▾

◯ **Individual territories** What are Individual Territory rights? ▾

I'd set it to be All Territories worldwide so you are available in all the countries:

Kindle eBook

LIVE Updates in review ▾

Submitted on

$9.99 USD

View on Amazon ▾

KINDLE EBOOK

> US > UK > DE > FR > ES > IT > NL > JP > BR > CA
> MX > AU > IN

Paperback

ROYALTIES AND PRICING

You can see immediately what price you set and what you will get out of it.
Amazon also has a **View Service** button to show you what books "similar to
yours" are selling for as well:

Royalty and Pricing

KDP Pricing Support (Beta)
See the relationship between price and past sales and author earnings for KDP books like yours.

[View Service]

Select a royalty plan and set your Kindle eBook list prices below

○ 35%
◉ 70%

i Your book file size after conversion is 2.46 MB.

Primary Marketplace	List Price		Rate	Delivery	Royalty
Amazon.com ⇕	$ 6.99	USD	35% ▾	$0.00	$2.45
	Must be $2.99-$9.99 ▾ All marketplaces are based on this price		70%	$0.37	$4.63

Out of $6.99 USD you would get $4.63 USD. You don't want to price too
low, nor too high. Somewhere between $4.99 and $9.99 seems to be a sweet
spot.

They also have a section for other marketplaces where you can see your
prices around the world:

Other Marketplaces (12)

Amazon.in	₹ 449	INR	₹381 without IN VAT	70%	₹17	₹254
	Must be ₹49-₹10999 ▾ Based on Amazon.com					
Amazon.co.uk	£ 5.31	GBP		70%	£0.25	£3.54
	Must be £1.77-£9.99 ▾ Based on Amazon.com					

BOOK LENDING & TERMS AND CONDITIONS

If you choose the 70% royalty option, you cannot unlock book lending:

Book Lending

Allow Kindle Book Lending (Optional)

Allow your customers to lend your Kindle eBook after purchasing it to their friends and family for a duration of 14 days. Learn more about Kindle Book Lending.

✓ Allow lending for this book Why is this locked? ▾

Terms & Conditions

It can take up to 72 hours for your title to be available for purchase on Amazon.

By clicking Publish below, I confirm that I have all rights necessary to make the content I am uploading available for marketing, distribution and sale in each territory I have indicated above, and that I am in compliance with the KDP Terms and Conditions.

If you chose the 35% option, you could remove the book lending option.

When you're ready, GO FOR IT!

| Save as Draft | Publish Your Kindle eBook |

Setup Printed Paperback Details

If you've already done the eBook section first, you can just skim through the info, and click **Save and Continue**.

It copies all of the information in. If you haven't done that or just want to do a **Printed** book, please refer back to the section **Setup Kindle eBook details**.

The only thing that is different is you have **Large Print** as an option.

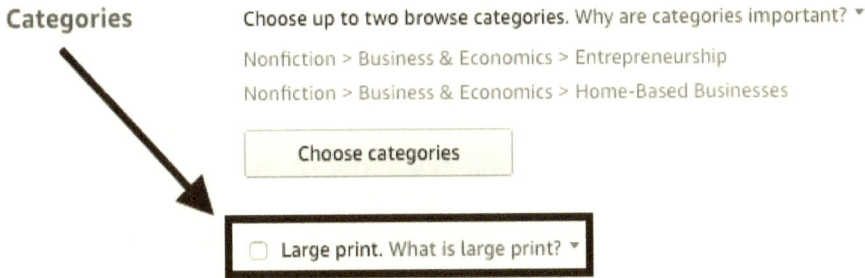

Setup Paperback Content

PRINT ISBN

So easy. You get a free ISBN assigned from Amazon:

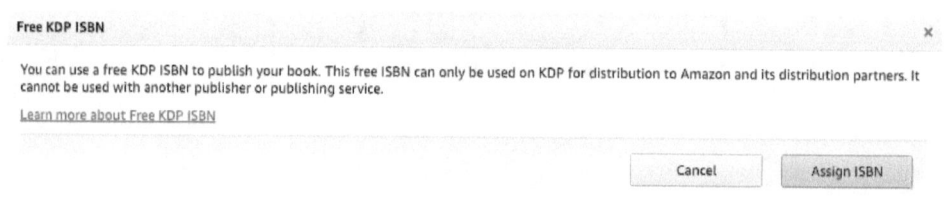

The only catch is the ISBN can only be used with Amazon and their partners, and if you go with another publishing company, you will need another ISBN (you can buy them actually, in packs of 10).

You should see this number:

Free KDP ISBN   ✕

You can use a free KDP ISBN to publish your book. This free ISBN can only be used on KDP for distribution to Amazon and its distribution partners. It cannot be used with another publisher or publishing service.

Learn more about Free KDP ISBN

Cancel   Assign ISBN

✓ Your book has been assigned a free KDP ISBN:

ISBN: 9798644811540

Imprint: Independently published

PUBLICATION DATE

You are publishing for the first time, so no need to set a date, leave it blank.

The options that are here, are perfectly fine:

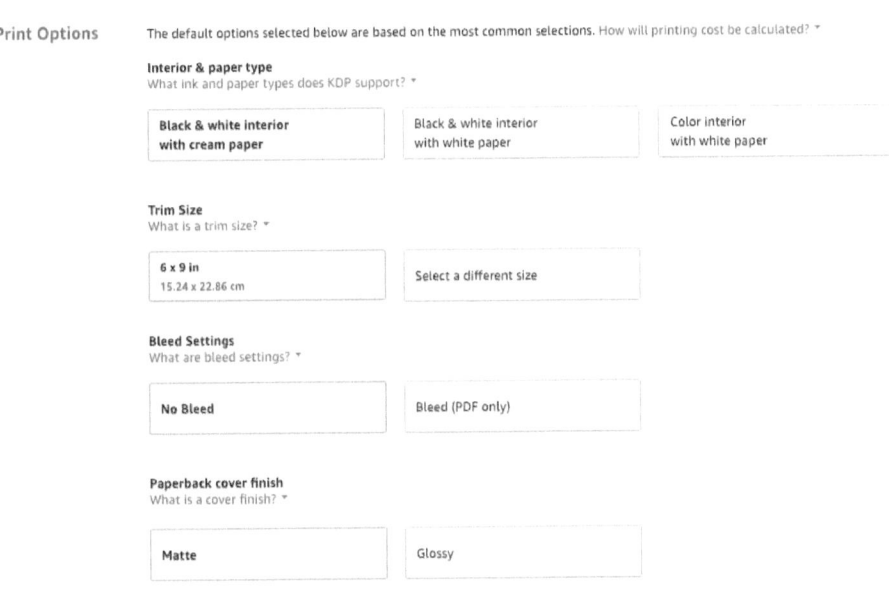

If you are using my templates, don't change a thing if you don't want to, except maybe to have cream versus white paper.

MANUSCRIPT

To upload a manuscript for a printed book, you can try .doc, .docx, .html, .rtf but the best one is PDF.

Convert your documents into PDF files and then upload them.

How to convert your book into PDF (MS Word)

Menu —> File —> Save As

Then at the bottom, look at the different formats you can save them in:

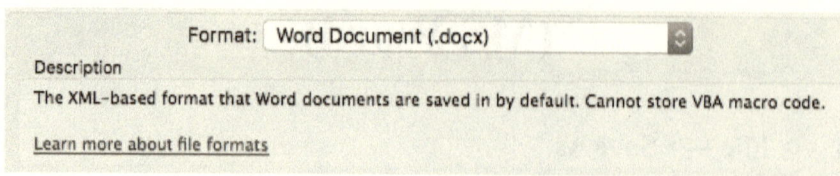

Format: Word Document (.docx)

Description
The XML-based format that Word documents are saved in by default. Cannot store VBA macro code.

Learn more about file formats

And save it as PDF:

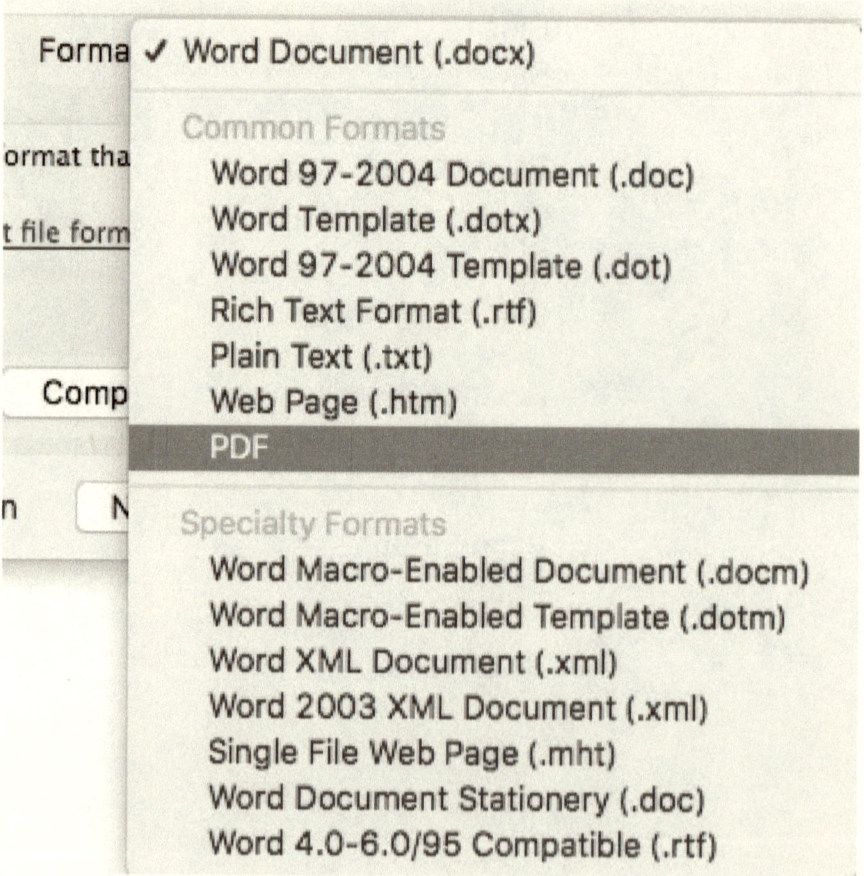

Forma ✓ Word Document (.docx)

Common Formats
ormat tha   Word 97-2004 Document (.doc)
             Word Template (.dotx)
t file form   Word 97-2004 Template (.dot)
             Rich Text Format (.rtf)
             Plain Text (.txt)
   Comp   Web Page (.htm)
             PDF

n   N   Specialty Formats
             Word Macro-Enabled Document (.docm)
             Word Macro-Enabled Template (.dotm)
             Word XML Document (.xml)
             Word 2003 XML Document (.xml)
             Single File Web Page (.mht)
             Word Document Stationery (.doc)
             Word 4.0-6.0/95 Compatible (.rtf)

How to convert your book into PDF (Pages Mac)

Menu —> File —> Export To —> PDF

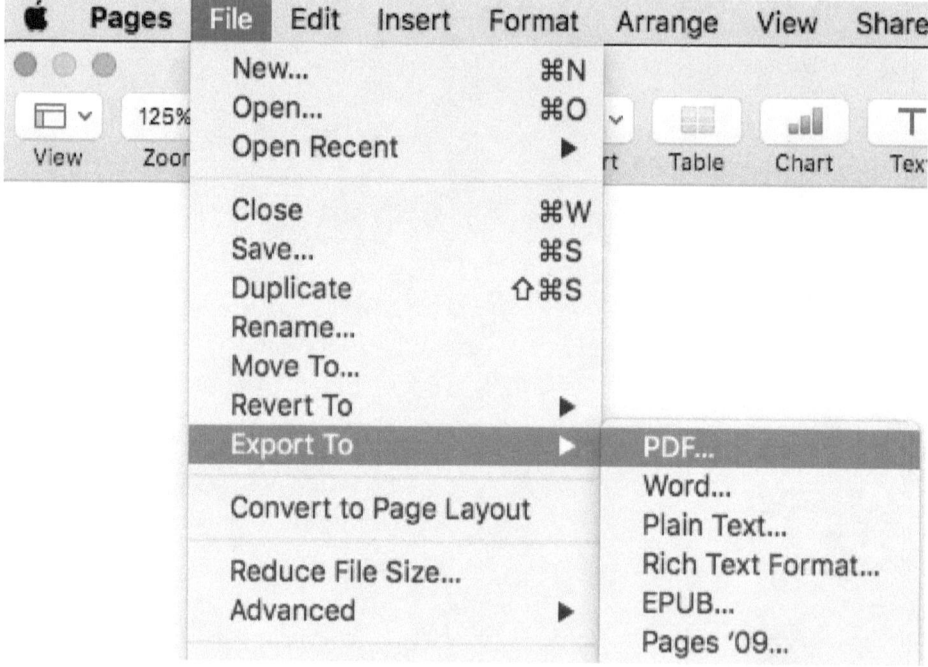

Select quality as **Best** and save it:

What also helps is naming it like you did with the others: NO COVER PDF

Save As: blish a Book Like a Boss NO COVER PDF   ^

Tags:

So it is easy to see the versions you have on your desktop.

How do I delete a book?

Once you create a book or get started and save it, you CANNOT DELETE THE BOOK from the Bookshelf.

You can however, filter through what you have Published or in Draft, which means you can see what you have Live or not.

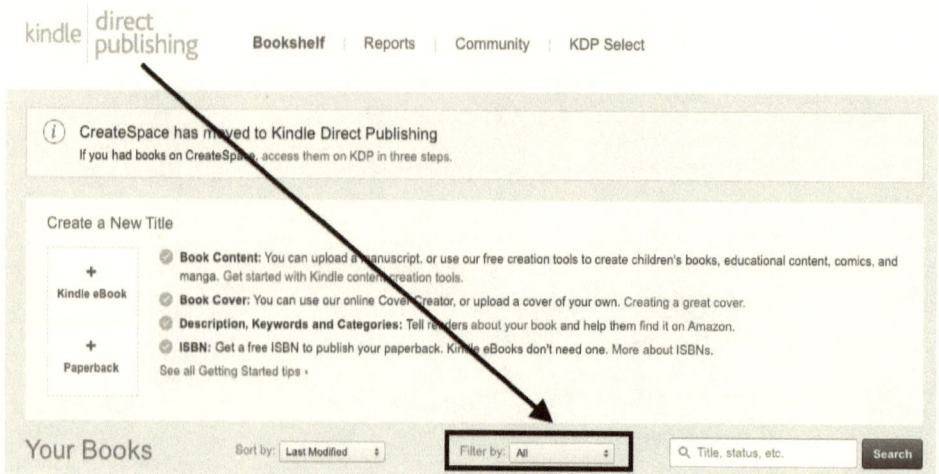

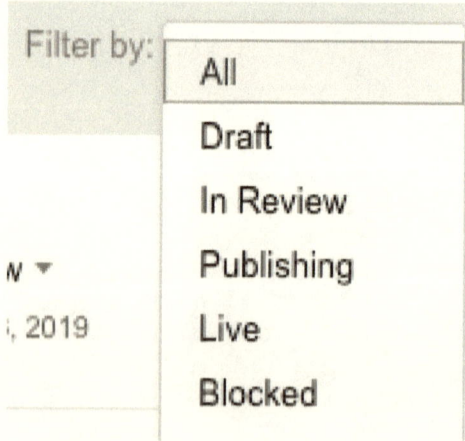

Live means what is published on Amazon and available for sale. That's the best.

I made a bunch of mistakes (test books, really) and when I discovered I couldn't delete them, I simply just repurposed them by renaming them and redoing the manuscript and cover images for my subsequent books.

That's another way to "delete them".

Really though, it's just aesthetics. Amazon doesn't care if you have 100 unpublished books that were drafts, it makes no difference to them.

Set up your Author Page

You have another page to go to for Author Central (https://authorcentral.amazon.com/gp/home) and set up your author page with pictures and a short bio.

You can edit your biography here:

I am a wealth-obsessed, style-focused, minimalist who blogs over at Save. Spend. Splurge. and basically spends the rest of my free time on Instagram (@saverspender).

I got out of $60,000 of debt in 18 months with The Budgeting Tool (TheBudgetingTool.com) which I now sell online and donate its net proceeds to charity, along with The Investing Tool.

Now, a little over a decade later, I am almost at $1M in personal net worth and reached financial independence/work-optional status at 35 meaning I don't need to work, and my side incomes are enough to cover my living expenses and to save.

I only work 50% of the time and when I do, I earn like a princess when I do work at my job but am trying hard to live like a duchess instead by not spending all of it because I am bougie and I know it.

My favourite day is payday, and my star sign is the $.

The rest of the time I relax and enjoy the time off by being with Little Bun (my rambunctious, ever-hungry little boy), blogging, eating...
» Read More

You can add your blog and your most recent posts will show up:

For your Author Page URL, get a custom one if you can:

This is important because you can see the actual Amazon Profile URL is: https://www.amazon.com/Sherry-H./e/B07XFQZBFN

When users type in: http://www.amazon.com/author/saverspender it takes them to that Author Page.

Add your books to your Author Page

Your book has to be published first.

amazon AuthorCentral   Author Page   **Books**   Sales Info ˅   Customer Reviews   Help   Sherry H. ˅

Books by Sherry H.

These are the books on Amazon's Sherry H. page ⬀. Click on any book below to view additional product details or submit corrections.

Are we missing a book?
If a book you've written does not appear in the selection below, you may add it now. Please note that only one edition of each work is shown in this list. Click an edition to make sure all related editions are also listed.

[Add more books]

Click on **Books** in the tab, and then click on **Add my books** and search for it. Once added, it will show up on your list:

Managing Money Like a Boss: The Money Management Picture Book: A Guide on how to take charge of your personal finances. Money is not boring and investing is easy!
2 Editions
Current Sales Rank: #1,247,512 in Books
Average Review: There are no reviews yet

Start a Blog Like a Boss: A Step-by-Step Method with Screenshots on how to To Launch Your Blog, Build A Loyal Readership and work from home: How to make real money blogging, not just pennies
2 Editions
Current Sales Rank: #6,083,016 in Books
Average Review: ⭐⭐⭐⭐⭐ (1 review)

Coming soon

The following book was recently added and will appear on the Author Page within 5 days.

Instagram Level Up Like a Boss: The DIY Guide to Secret Tips & Tricks
2 Editions

Add detail to your books

Click on each book and add more detail to each, this is kind of like your own personal bookshelf on Amazon:

Start a Blog Like a Boss: A Step-by-Step Method with Screenshots on how to To Launch Your Blog, Build A Loyal Readership and work from home: How to make real money blogging, not just pennies
Paperback

ASIN: 1690147393
ISBN-13: 978-1690147398
Average Review: ☆☆☆☆☆ (1 reviews)
Current Sales Rank: #6,083,016 in Books
View on Amazon.com

Editions
Paperback
Kindle Edition   (Kindle eBook)

Editorial Reviews   Book Details

Review   Edit
Janelle: "As someone who has been blogging for a number of years I know I have made every mistake imaginable. If only Start A Blog Like A Boss: How To Make Money had been around when I started blogging, I would have saved myself a whole lot of time, money and grief. Sherry has the perfect advice for new bloggers - but she also provides great tips for experienced bloggers who are looking to start monetising their blogs. And it's all delivered in a format that is easy to read and follow! Thank you Sherry for creating a fabulous resource."

Review   Edit
Paulin: "This is an amazing resource for newbies. I like the fact that you added a tutorial on how to actually set up the blog itself; this is an important tech-related step that most "how to" guide forget to include. Very detailed and I like it. Also great expert advice regarding picking a permalink structure."

You can talk a bit about yourself, add reviews that weren't from Amazon, and more detail on each book.

TOOLS

Designing a Book Cover

You could use a free-rights image, and one of my favourite sites for this is Unsplash (http://unsplash.com/) and put some text over it.

You can use any of those images for free personal and commercial usage.

If you don't have an image editor your options are as follows:

Adobe Photoshop - $21 USD/month

https://www.adobe.com/products/photoshop.html

The holy grail of all editors, but very expensive.

Pixelmator - $30 USD

https://www.pixelmator.com/mac/

Great image editor for Mac OS systems

Paint.Net - $0

https://www.getpaint.net/download.html

Easy to learn image editor for the PC

GIMP - $0

https://www.gimp.org/downloads/

Image editor for Mac OS, PC or Linux

You want to make sure you make the biggest book cover image possible with the highest resolution otherwise the image won't print clearly and look professional.

Your other option is to let Amazon create it for you.

Choose from Amazon Cover Colours

This is what you have to work with and you can download this in the files

I would strongly recommend picking from this limited palette of colours as it will make creating the book cover for your book a lot easier.

You don't need to only use these colours in the cover, but at least use it for your background cover/all over the book, so it can blend in easier when you create your cover. You'll see what I mean when I get into creating it for Print.

Each of these colours swatches has a unique HEX colour code.

A HEX colour code is the 6 character code for that exact shade, and tone. When you say for instance "000000" it means black. When you say "FFFFFF" it means white. It's how people know how to match the exact colour without guessing in an image editor.

Unfortunately, Amazon allows only a set palette of HEX code colours (that grid you see), and they don't let you enter HEX colour codes in Amazon.

So the method is to take the colour background you want from Amazon's grid as shown, get the HEX code in your image editor then work your background/cover image in your image editing program, and then when you go to build your Cover in Amazon, remember which square you picked to take the original HEX colour code from, and set it as the background colour so it all blends in.

Create the eBook Cover in Amazon

You only need the front cover image for the book, and then just upload it. You don't need a back cover page at all.

For eBook creation, you want to simply **Upload that cover file** you created under the Cover Creator part:

Create the Print Cover in Amazon

For print, you will want to use **Cover Creator** with the front cover image.

You should use their Cover Creator instead of trying to create an image file that fits perfectly for a Print Book, and making sure all the elements line up together and don't block the barcode, etc.

You can TRY to create a flat cover in a PDF format like this but to get it perfectly positioned so that the spine shows the title, the subtitle, the barcode section, etc… it is exhaustingly mind-numbing and unnecessary work you don't need to undertake.

To do this the fast and dirty way, make sure you have your cover image (with the background from one of the chosen Amazon palette colours as mentioned in the cover book considerations section).

Go into Cover Creator and upload the Cover Image from your computer:

You can see a bunch of options but the easiest is the one on the left:

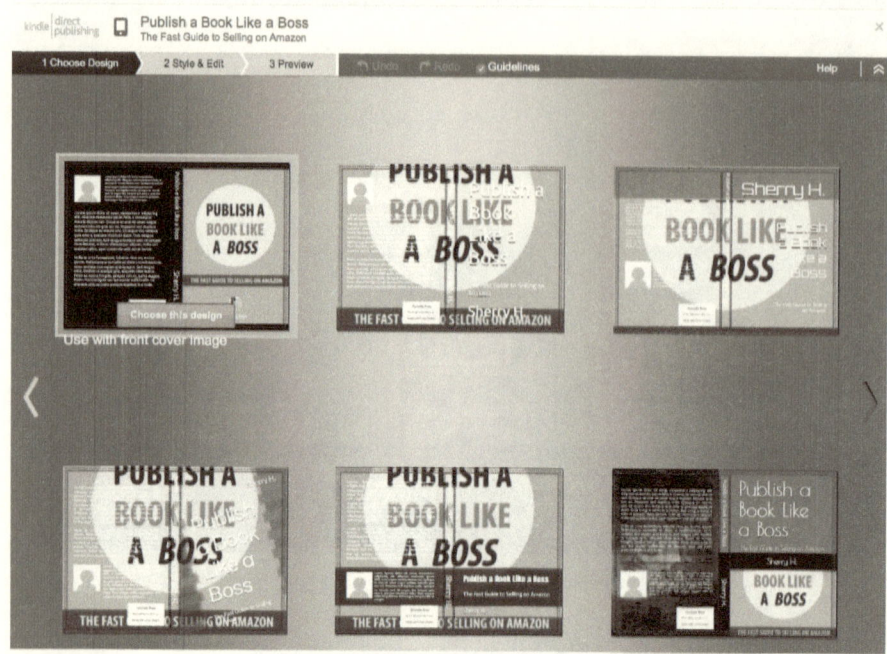

This one, lets you have a cover, and then you just change the background to match, add your blurb and it's ready to go!

Now you can select the colours at the bottom menu:

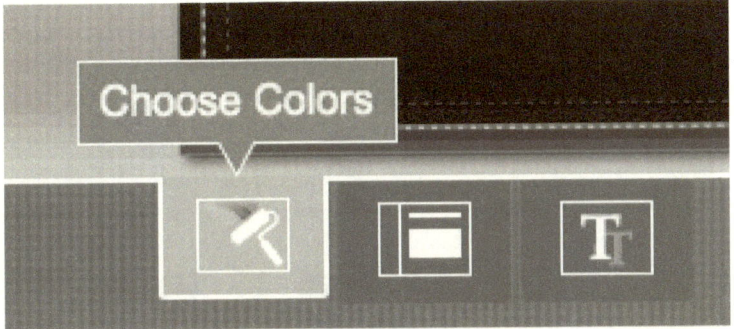

This is where that colour palette from Amazon came in handy before, you have to just select the colour that you used for the background:

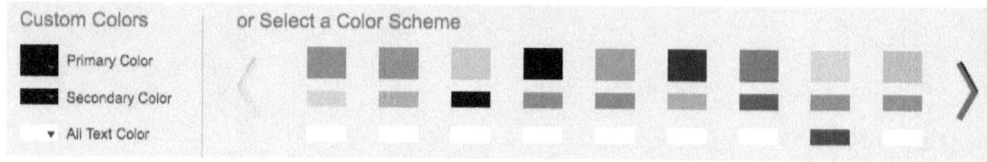

You can see once I changed it to the blue I chose, it looks almost finished, it was so much easier than trying to create the cover & then find an Amazon background cover colour to match!

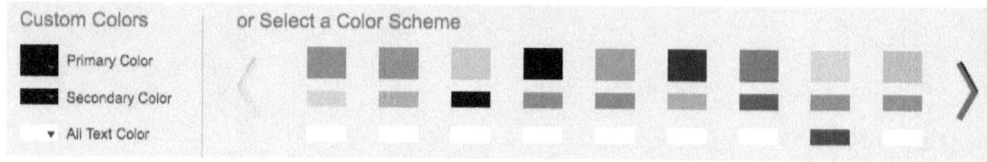

Now you need to fill in the author picture (you don't have to use your photo of yourself, but use whatever you're using on your Author Central Amazon Page):

Want to become a published author within a day?

Sherry of Save. Spend. Splurge. has published the Like a Boss book series, and shares her quickstart guide, tips and tricks on how to get published on Amazon digitally and in print.

Assuming your content is written, it's quite easy to become published if you have the templates and the ins-and-outs of what to do and what not to do.

Included with the book are all the extras such as template sizes for books in two formats (MS Word and Pages for Mac), formatting notes to save you hours of headache and stress because if you start the foundation out correctly, you won't have to do so much rework, and all the technical and helpful shortcuts.

Barcode Area

We will add the barcode for you.

Made with Cover Creator

Publish a Book Like a Boss

Sherry H.

PUBLISH A BOOK LIKE A BOSS

THE FAST GUIDE TO SELLING ON AMAZON

BY SHERRY

Spend some time on the blurb on yourself at the back and try to say something different than from the book description itself on the page.

The bottom right area has now an empty spot for **Barcode Area** and is perfect for when the book is printed and it will print just like this. Now click on **Preview** to see it in full:

You can see the jacket without any lines now:

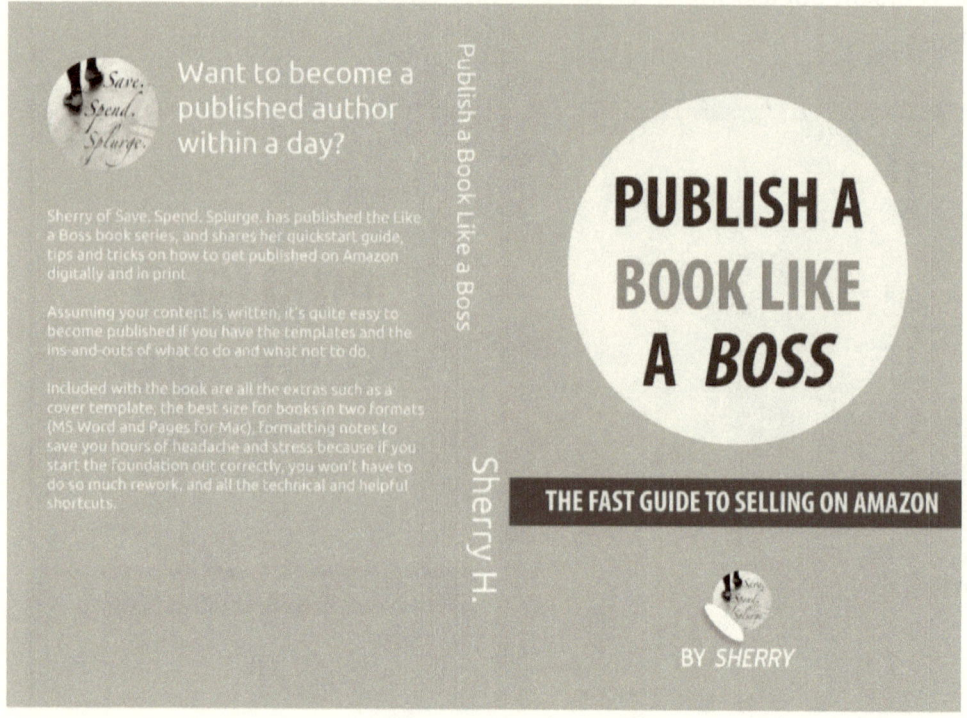

Now you can just **Save & Submit** and you're finished!

Trim Sizes you need

Everything is converted from inches to millimetres.

6X9 = 152.4 mm x 228.6 mm as shown below is the **most common size for a book** as it is a paperback size.

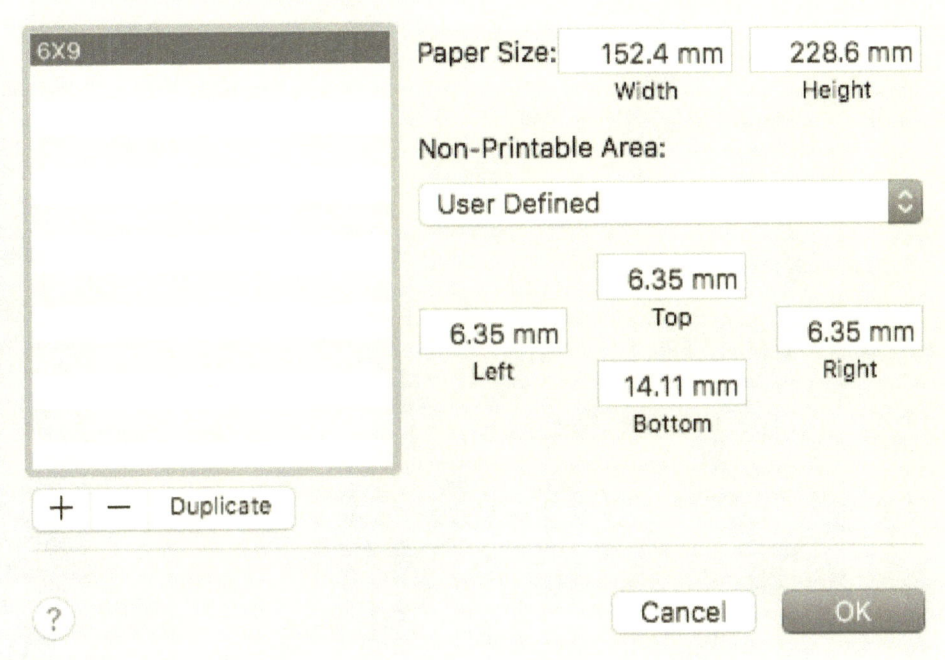

If you want another trim size for a larger or smaller book (based on the standard sizes Amazon offers), you will need to convert from inches to millimetres for your paper size/page setup as a custom size.

Amazon offers the following trim sizes for books:

Trim size
5" x 8" (12.7 x 20.32 cm)
5.06" x 7.81" (12.85 x 19.84 cm)
5.25" x 8" (13.34 x 20.32 cm)
5.5" x 8.5" (13.97 x 21.59 cm)
6" x 9" (15.24 x 22.86 cm)
6.14" x 9.21" (15.6 x 23.39 cm)
6.69" x 9.61" (16.99 x 24.41 cm)
7" x 10" x (17.78 x 25.4 cm)
7.44" x 9.69" (18.9 x 24.61 cm)
7.5" x 9.25" (19.05 x 23.5 cm)
8" x 10" (20.32 x 25.4 cm)
8.25" x 6" (20.96 x 15.24 cm)
8.25" x 8.25" (20.96 x 20.96 cm)
8.5" x 8.5" (21.59 x 21.59 cm)
8.5" x 11" (21.59 x 27.94 cm)
8.27" x 11.69" (21 x 29.7 cm)

Remember, the bigger the book or less common the size, the more money it costs to produce/print it in many cases.

Also, don't forget to convert the centimetres shown in the Amazon trim size chart to millimetres when you do your Page Setup for custom sizes.

OTHER

Doing Ebook & Print

You should definitely sell in both ebook and print, as some people prefer the written word over a digital file.

To easily transition, you don't necessarily need to copy and paste all the content into the second format for print let's say, but you could just adjust the margins based on what they should be for ebook or print.

Instructions on how to do that are under **PUBLISH** on how to adjust the Trim Size and Document Margins and set up your proper Page Setup for the document size.

So technically you could take your finished ebook, do a quick once-over to check to make sure the formatting hasn't screwed up anything, and save that as your PRINT copy.

Publish a Book Like a Boss NO COVER EBOOK
Publish a Book Like a Boss NO COVER PRINT

My core files look like the above, and I save an EPUB version of the EBOOK file, and the PDF version for the PRINT file to upload as my Amazon manuscripts.

ALWAYS make sure once you look back over your work because things will need to be adjusted (words may end up cut off, or on the side of images). I'd do this when you have time, aren't rushed, and relaxed. First impressions make a big deal and you don't want to release a shoddily produced piece of work.

Marketing

Some ideas of what you could do to make sure your books are marketed, is to create a website, a blog, and/or social media profiles (Facebook, Instagram, Tumblr, Pinterest, etc).

A website is a great way, especially if you blog, to have people hear your voice, like your writing, and then want to buy your books.

At the very, VERY least, set up some social media profiles to tweet, and post on Instagram for instance to get your name out there, your book, your ideas.

For anyone who buys your book, asking them to leave reviews on Amazon would be GOLD, and don't be afraid to solicit feedback or some help in this.

You're a new author with no publishing powerhouse of marketing, book signings, presenting the author, TV shows, etc — none of that is happening, you have to build up momentum the grassroots way.

The best way? Blog, Website, Social Media. Even Etsy, to sell digital copies of the book is a option.

In many ways it is a another round of work to get your book marketed and to have people buying your books and reading them, than the work it was to actually write the book.

If not, how will anyone but your family and friends see it? Make sure you have a marketing plan of some sort set up before you publish a book.

THE END

All of this has been a whirlwind of self-teaching, experimenting and trying out new ideas to see what worked and what didn't.

I made SO. MANY. MISTAKES. and spent hours trying to create covers, format books, edit everything to make it perfect for ALL tablets and ALL e-readers and formats.

It really was a lot of stress for nothing when you realize at the end, only a few things matter when it comes to publishing.

I hope this book has helped shortcut a lot of what happens behind the scenes and how publishing works, and the tips and tricks to make it work.

Drop me a line any time:

Sherry@SaveSpendSplurge.com

I'd love to hear from you!

(Really.)

ABOUT THE AUTHOR

Sherry is a 30-something professional entrepreneur who lives in Canada with her partner and toddler (whom she has affectionately nicknamed *Little Bun* on the blog).

She has been blogging for more than 10 years having started with clearing $60,000 of student debt in 18 months using *The Budgeting Tool*

(**TheBudgetingTool.com**) which she now donates the net proceeds of to charity) to quadrupling her yearly income within two years of graduation and investing using *The Investing Tool* (**TheInvestingTool.com**).

This is the fifth book she has authored in the **LikeaBossBooks.com** series, and she has plans for many more.

She is work-optional meaning she doesn't need her job's paycheque any more, but loves it enough to keep going. Her side incomes bring in almost $50K a year now.

Sherry loves those rare, uninterrupted nights of deep REM sleep, stuffing her face with delicious food, and pretending she isn't secretly addicted to blogging and shopping for winter coats. You can read more about this wealth-focused, style-obsessed, minimalist at her latest blog *Save. Spend. Splurge.* (**SaveSpendSplurge.com**).

Sherry@LikeABossBooks.com

@saverspender

Thank you!

www.ingramcontent.com/pod-product-compliance
Lightning Source LLC
Chambersburg PA
CBHW020543220526
45463CB00006B/2173